Thanks

William Lee Golden

WILLIAM LEE GOLDEN

Behind the Beard

The Autobiography
with Scot England

Behind the Beard – The Autobiography by William Lee Golden with Scot England

ISBN: 9780998636788-

Copyright 2021 England Media

Editor: Steve Jenne
Layout: Paula Underwood Winters
Cover Photo/Design: Alan Messer
www.williamleegoldenbook.com Website Design:
Renae Johnson

Printed in the United States of America

For more info on William Lee Golden, visit
www.williamleegolden.com

Published by:
England Media
102 Rachels Ct
Hendersonville TN 37075

If you enjoyed this book, you will also like these autobiographies published by England Media:

Misty Rowe "Misty Memories"
Lulu Roman "This Is My Story; This Is My Song"
Jimmy Capps "The Man in Back"
Ronnie McDowell "Bringing It to You Personally"
Johnny Lee "Still Lookin' for Love"
Moe Bandy "Lucky Me"
Larry Black "The Cameras Weren't Always Rollin'"

CONTENTS

DEDICATION

I dedicate this book to:

My Mother and Father, and also to my Grandparents. They all encouraged me and made feel that what I was doing really meant something.

My sons. Rusty, Craig, Chris and Solomon all grew up with a father who was away from home 200 to 250 days a year. I missed out on a lot of special life events, but each of my sons grew up to be men I am very proud of.

My partners, Richard, Duane and Joe, and also to the managers, agents and concert promoters who helped make the Oak Ridge Boys a household name.

The fans. This book is for every fan who ever bought a concert ticket, purchased a record or took the time to ask for an autograph. Without you, this book would not have happened.

My best friend, Jeff Panzer. I'll be there for you until the day I die, Jeff.

My co-writer, Scot England. You have been a great guy through all this. I know this book would not have happened without your persistence and your insistence that I had a story that was worth telling.

My wife, Simone. You have been there with a patient support during everything I have tried to do. You have believed in my visions, and I believe in you.

— WLG

When you write your life story, and you decide to bare everything, it's kind of scary. It feels a lot like getting naked…in front of the entire world. Now that I've committed to it, there is one thing going through my mind…if I was going to get naked in front of everyone, I probably shouldn't have waited until I was 82 years old!

FOREWORD

"William Lee Golden is a lot of different things to a lot of different people. But he is a person who knows who he is. He is a man of integrity and honesty. You will read his very honest words in this book.

If you are lucky, you might have ten people in your life who were really influential, and the relationship you had was so substantial that it showed that you really cared for each other. William is one of those people in my life.

The Oak Ridge Boys truly are like a family. We've all had a very close relationship for many decades. It is rare in this business to not only have a close business relationship, but also a close personal relationship. When you can combine those two, you can make some magic, and the Oak Ridge Boys have made some magic over the years.

There are certain people who magically come together. There was a bonding that William and I had that goes beyond any type of business relationship. We meshed like family. William, Richard, Duane and Joe all treated my late son Sherman like a brother, and I love all of William's boys, who are now all grown men. Since I lost my son, I kind of look at his kids as my surrogate sons.

This book tells the story of a man who has dedicated his life to helping people. His songs have healed people. I love William. He is so kind, especially to the fans, and I think 'Thank God for Kids' is one of the most recognizable songs in country music. His solo on that song still gets one of the biggest responses of any in their show.

All the Oak Ridge Boys have a mission. That mission is to try to make people's lives better. The four guys do that each night they are on stage. For two hours, through something that is true magic, they are able to take away every worry and care that audience has. Every person in the crowd has peace, harmony, and joy for a couple hours, and during these crazy times, that is something that takes true magic to accomplish. And the audience members take that joy with them when they leave the concert, and months and even years later, they can think back to that night, and they can get a little bit of that great feeling again.

All the Oaks believe in the same thing. We all worship God, and we all believe we have a duty and obligation to help our fellow man. William Lee and the Oak Ridge Boys have done that all their lives, and they continue to do it.

There is nobody better in the world than William Lee Golden."

— Jim Halsey/Manager, Oak Ridge Boys

AN ACORN (LITTLE NUT) IS BORN

Our Golden family story started long before I was born. There were numerous important and impressive people in my family tree. So, allow me to go back quite a few years before I came along.

The Golden family owned the foundry in Columbus, Georgia. They made cannon balls that were used in the Civil War. My great grandfather fought the entire Civil War in heavy artillery. He fired off some of the same cannon balls his family members had made in Columbus. From the age of 18 to 21, my great grandfather fought in 8 major Civil War battles. Those included the battles of Nashville, Franklin, Vicksburg and Atlanta. He survived them all.

My mother was a quiet woman. Her name was Ruth, but when my son Rusty was a little boy, he had a hard time saying "Grandma," and instead, he called her "Gaggie." From that point on, for the rest of her life, all our family called her Gaggie.

Mother was shy and timid, the opposite of my dad. I'm sure I got my shyness from my mother. Mother expressed herself through writings and poetry. She loved poetry, and she wrote poems from the time she was a girl. She once wrote a poem for her mother, and I saved it over the years. When mother died in 2008, at the age of 91, we thought that poem also fit her, so we put it on her tombstone.

Mother was raised a Latter Day Saint, and she had a powerful impact on me. She cared for all of us, and I still remember when she would warm bricks in the fireplace. Then she wrapped the bricks up in cloth and put them on our feet, to keep us warm in bed on cold nights. Mother and daddy were very unselfish. They were always giving to their children, their family, and friends.

My dad's story is phenomenal in itself. He was one of 12 children in his family. He was the 9th child, and he was a triplet. Dad and his brothers were identical triplets. Dad was named Luke and his brothers were Matthew and Mark. Dad was the last of the three to be born, and he always joked that he was the "runt of the bunch." While he was born small in stature, his two brothers had more serious health issues, that began with a lack of nutrition. My grandma was very small, and she couldn't feed all of her newborn sons. That caused Luke, Matthew and Mark to each develop spinal meningitis. Matthew died at the age of 7 months and Mark passed away just two months later.

Our family expected Luke to also die, especially since he was littler than the other boys who had passed. But Luke somehow survived. My father always wondered why he was the one who was allowed to live out his life. If he had died, you wouldn't be holding this book right now, because there would never have been a William Lee Golden. My dad lived to be 75 years old.

My grandfather moved from Talapoosa County, Alabama, east of Montgomery to the Brewton area, and bought a large farm right on the Alabama and Florida state line. Brewton's main business was the timber industry, and there were a number of big lumber yards in the area. But my family were farmers. Farming was passed down to my father from his father.

My grandfather, Lee Rush Golden, helped his sons and daughters purchase as much farmland as they could around the Brewton area. My dad had dreamed of owning 40 acres of land

and a pair of mules. But his first farm was actually 80 acres, and yes, he did farm those 80 with just two mules.

Daddy worked just as hard as his mules, and his hard work paid off as his farm grew to 1, 200 acres. Around Brewton, his acreage was second only to his brother Ed, who farmed over 5, 000 acres in that same area. Those farms are still in our Golden name today, as Uncle Ed's sons and grandsons carry on the family tradition.

Granddaddy Golden was a very successful farmer, but he added another title to his resume when he got older. He became a preacher. He helped build a little church outside Brewton, and that church is still standing today. The Golden family cemetery is just a few steps from the church. It's where my parents and other family members are buried, and it will be my final resting place when that time comes.

As Luke and Ruth Golden rang in the new year of 1939, they prepared to celebrate by welcoming a new child to their family. On the evening of January 11, Doctor Tippin was called to my parents' two-room farm shack. Doc Tippin had delivered my sister Lanette in that same house four years earlier. By the way, many years later, while I was doing the "Nashville Now" TV show, country singer Aaron Tippin surprised me when he said, "William, do you know that my great grandfather is the person who delivered you?" Yes, Aaron's great grandfather was known to us as simply, "Doc Tippin." Doc also delivered my younger brother Ronnie.

While the doctor tended to mother as she began her labor, the temperature outside began to fall. My father put a little pallet of blankets near our stove, so Doc Tippin could warm up as he rested during the night. I would wait until the next morning at about 11:00 a.m. before I made my official debut.

Ol' Doc Tippin was quite surprised when I came out sporting a long white beard. (This is just a joke. I was wanting to make sure you were still paying attention!)

The home I was born in is long gone now. I only lived there for the first year of my life. When I was one, we moved a mile and a half away. But even though I was a little baby, I can still remember the rooms of that home. I can see it all in my mind, now over 80 years later.

It should come as no surprise that one of my earliest memories involves music. I can vividly recall listening to the Grand Ole Opry on a battery-operated radio. We had no electricity or running water, but we had a radio. I'd turn that radio up loud and sit in awe as I listened to the audience going crazy as they watched the Opry stars like Little Jimmy Dickens perform. It was magical. Listening to the Opry on the radio really was magic for a little boy, and it made a huge impact on me.

Our home was as far south as you can go in the state of Alabama. If I walked for just a few minutes, I would be in Florida. We were also as far out in the country and as far away from civilization as you can get. I was very sheltered from "the real world" as I was growing up.

Our farm was next to a big forest and I grew up in those woods. I became an outdoorsman at a very young age. Back in those heavy woods, I was like a miniature Tarzan. I learned early on to always be on the lookout for poisonous snakes, like the rattlers, copperheads, cotton mouths and water moccasins. There were huge snakes in those woods, but I didn't mind.

A few years later, I had what could have been a deadly encounter with one of those snakes. Our school bus hit a King snake, and I jumped out of the bus and went to catch it. The snake was injured and scared, and when I went to grab it, the snake bit me hard on the arm. I grabbed him with my other hand and pulled him off.

Spending most of my time, playing in the woods, was the most wonderful way to grow up. Living off the land gave me confidence that I could survive anything. I was a wide-eyed little kid, in wonderment of everything, and I still have that same wonderment today.

But that wonder turned to terror when I was four years old. We were so far out in the country, that I rarely saw anyone who wasn't an immediate family member. But one day, I was out in the woods, pretending to be a cowboy or Indian, when I heard the sound of hundreds of gunshots. Then I saw tanks and Army men marching right toward me. It scared me to death.

I ran inside and my mother explained that it was the Army, doing maneuvers and military exercises in the woods by our house. With the big Naval station, Whiting Field not far from us, and the Pensacola Naval Air Station also close by, the tanks and troops would come through quite often. All the Navy was training in our backyard!

Things were extra frightening when fast moving and very low flying military aircraft started coming toward our home. The pilots used the tiny Brewton airport to practice "touch-and-go's," so they could learn how to land on aircraft carriers. Of course, the Army wanted to do their training away from populated areas, but they ended up right where we lived. I'd be out in the woods, trying to catch a frog, while hundreds of heavily armed military men were practicing war games.

When I was six years old, we moved to a larger house, up the road. Our home didn't have electricity until I was 8 years old. We chopped wood and cooked with a wood stove. We had to pump water and bring it in from outside. Back then, most home fires started in the kitchen, so our kitchen was in a separate building a few steps away from our main house.

Before getting into farming, my dad worked in a shipyard. When I was a toddler, dad would leave home before daylight and wouldn't return until well after dark. But daddy gave his notice at the shipyard after he found his true passion…farming. He had a passion for farming like I have a passion for singing. And he never lost his passion for farming. He loved it all his life. He'd get up early each morning and work hard all day, until late at night.

To say that we were "poor farmers" would be an understatement. After farming with just two mules, daddy saved up enough money to buy a tractor. That was all we had during the first ten years of my life. Then we got a pickup truck, but we had a tractor before we had any other form of transportation.

We may have been poor, but dad made sure that was no excuse for his children not to get an education. While a lot of kids missed school so they could help their family farm, daddy wouldn't let us miss school. But as soon as we got home, we were expected to work on the farm most of the evening. Our first job was to feed and milk the cows, before I headed toward our fields. I spent a large part of my childhood and teen years picking cotton and peanuts. I picked cotton by hand, but I was a terrible cotton picker. Everybody else could pick more than me. I also had to hoe the grass and weeds out of the field.

My father supported my music and singing, but he wanted me to farm. He said I could sing while I was in the field, working. But there was no way I would be allowed to stay in the house and play guitar all day when there was a field full of peanuts and cotton that needed taken care of.

I enjoyed watching my father as his business got larger, and as he accomplished things in his life. My dad taught me the value of hard work, but he also taught me even more important lessons. He taught us that everyone is special. He also instructed his children how to be honest and how to treat everybody fairly.

He taught us integrity and lived by the motto, "If your word is no good, your signature on a contract is no good."

Dad was a strict disciplinarian. If I did something wrong, I knew that I would be punished for it. I am thankful for the discipline my father dealt out. I became a better person because of it. My mother and dad loved me, and I could feel that love, even when I was being punished.

My dad never met a stranger. He was outgoing and could talk to anyone. Dad had a great appreciation for life, and he passed that on to all his kids. My parents had so many friends, and they welcomed them all into our home. We always had people coming and going when I was growing up.

Music was also a big part of our home. In addition to listening to the Opry on the radio, we also enjoyed making our own music. That started when my mother was singing Roy Acuff's "Great Speckled Bird." My sister Lanette was just 3 years old, but she began singing perfect alto harmony with mother.

Mother and Daddy gave Lanette music and piano lessons, and when I was 5 years old, Lanette taught me how to harmonize with her as she played the piano. My confidence grew as my sister told me, "William, you have a natural gift. You have an ear for harmony." Of course, my voice hadn't changed yet, and Lanette sang in a lower key than I did. Today, when people compliment the Oak Ridge Boys on our harmonies, I always think back to the person who first taught me how to sing harmony…my sister Lanette.

Mother played the harmonica, and her brothers were also quite musical. They sang the popular songs of the day as they played different instruments. Uncle Jake played mandolin, harmonica, guitar and piano. I'm sure I got most of my musical talent from my mother's side of the family. My dad always said, "The only thing I can play is the radio."

I developed a strong interest in music when I was a little boy. And my duets with Lanette got even more interesting when she started playing Uncle Jake's mandolin. Lanette was smart and seemed to naturally take to any musical instrument she picked up. She also mastered the guitar at a young age, and then began teaching me to play it. It seemed that her biggest challenge was just keeping my guitar in tune. With her perfect ear, she could tell when it was off, and she could have it back in tune just an instant after I handed it off to her.

My granddaddy Lee Golden and his brother Will both preached during a Sunday morning radio show on the local station, WEBJ. The show was called "The Old Country Church," and it would be the place where William Lee Golden made his public singing debut. I was 9 and Lanette was 13, when we sang one song live on the show each week. We did the show for over a year, and we tried to perform a different song each week.

Mother would teach us the gospel songs that some of the country stars had at the time. We learned Kitty Wells' "Mansion Over the Hilltop" and Hank Williams' "I Saw the Light." We also learned many of the songs the popular duo, the Louvin Brothers recorded, and we tried our best to match the Louvins' perfect harmonies. The Louvins also used a mandolin and Lanette told me if she kept practicing her mandolin and I got better on the rhythm guitar, that she was sure we could be as good as Ira and Charlie Louvin.

During his younger days, my granddad was a fiddle player and he performed at square dances and honky-tonks. Many years later, when I sang on his radio show, grandpa would talk about watching the audiences at the dances and honky-tonks. His face lit up as he described how he could see the music overtake the crowd. I was captivated by his vivid description, and it was then that I started to dream of the day that I might try to affect a crowd with my own music.

When I was 10 years old, my father bought Lanette a brand-new mandolin, and he bought me an F-hole Gibson guitar. Mother knew the G, C and D chords, and she showed me how to play those. Lanette taught me the rest. I played that guitar until I got out of high school, and I still have it today.

When Lanette became a teenager, she liked to buy the latest record albums. She usually bought the newest gospel quartet records, because she loved their harmony singing. Not that many young people were into gospel music, but I enjoyed singing the older spiritual songs. I still do.

Our entire family would listen as Lanette played the newest album on a record player we had in the corner of our living room. That original record player is now in my son Chris' living room. Daddy smiled in approval as he listened to the gospel records, and he could easily, by heart, quote different scriptures that went along with the songs that were playing. My father loved gospel and also enjoyed country music, but he didn't allow us to blare the new rock and roll songs that seemed to be taking over the radio airwaves.

For years, people have commented about me being quiet and laid back. I have been that way my entire life. I was not very outgoing, and my sister and my younger brother Ronnie were always more talkative than I was. Ronnie is four years younger than me, but he came very close to never making it into adulthood.

When he was four years old, for some reason, Ronnie went to school with me and Lanette. He hadn't started school yet, but he was allowed to ride the school bus with us. On the way home, as the bus was going down the highway at about 30 miles per hour, Ronnie got up to walk from one side of the bus to the other and he fell against the back door. The door wasn't locked, and Ronnie fell out of the moving bus. It is a miracle he didn't die. But God had more for Ronnie to do in life. He did break his leg. They took him to the hospital, where they had to drill holes into his thigh bone, and he was put in traction for quite a while. Once he was out of the hospital, I helped him get around and taught him how to use his crutches.

A few years later, there was a far-less serious incident on the school bus. But it was one I never forgot. I was 13 at the time, and I was constantly singing. One day, as the school bus driver did his best to get us all home safely, I began to sing…very loudly. At the top of my lungs, I belted out, "Zip-a-Dee-Doo-Dah! Zip-a-Dee-ay!"

It felt good to sing out loud, and I was enjoying myself. But all at once, the driver of that bus slammed on the brakes and came walking down the aisle. Before I could even get out, "My, Oh, My, What a Wonderful Day," the driver grabbed my shoulder and shouted, "If you don't shut your mouth, I'm gonna put you off this bus and you'll walk." That was the last time I serenaded my classmates on the way home.

I didn't mean to upset the bus driver. I just liked to have fun. While my brother and sister were both extremely smart and got good grades, I just wanted to enjoy myself in school. I found I could mimic people, and I could walk and talk like my teachers and classmates. I liked to be funny, and I'll be the first to admit that I didn't put much effort into my studies.

I always enjoyed my time at home much more than I did at school. My home was a quiet, peaceful place. We left our doors unlocked. We didn't even lock them at night. When I was a teenager, coming home late at night, I never had a key to our house. I always knew that the door would be open…and my parents would be waiting up for me.

I loved and respected my parents, and I just enjoyed being around my mom and dad and all our family. I never heard my parents argue. I was raised in a home where I never heard my mother or father use a curse word, in or out of the house. How many people can say that? My daddy didn't even cuss the day that I saw him madder than any other in his life. Unfortunately, I was the one he was mad at.

I had begun driving our family pickup when I was 14. I didn't have a driver's license, but that didn't stop me from driving everywhere. When Dad needed something in town, he'd tell me to drive in to pick it up. But one day when I was 15, I took a joyride that turned into anything but joyful.

Daddy, grandpa and grandma were going to a political rally. Grandpa left his truck at our house…with the keys in it. I had told dad that there was a peanut boil taking place not far away, but as he left for the rally, his last words to me were, "Don't leave the house."

Of course, as soon as they were out of sight, Ronnie, my cousin Marcus, and I all climbed into grandpa's truck. And of course, I was the one behind the wheel. We headed down the dirt road, through the woods. I was going at a pretty fast clip when I came to a sandbed that was at a curve in the road. At that moment, an old sow and some pigs ran out in front of us.

I whipped the steering wheel hard left and managed to miss the pigs. But when the back tires hit that sand, our truck began to slowly turn over. From that moment on, we were all just along for the ride. The truck flipped completely over and landed on its roof, and the entire top was caved in. The truck didn't have seatbelts, but somehow, we were not injured. We crawled out of the crashed truck, and then wondered how we were going to get home. The only thing we could do, was get the truck back on its wheels. So, just the three of us boys lifted the truck over to one side and then finally rolled it all the way back over. I drove my grandpa's badly dented pickup back home, where my dad gave me the hardest whippin' I ever got.

My brother Ronnie has had a very interesting and successful life. We are still quite close today. I thought this would be a good place to have him share a few of his memories of our younger days:

"Since I'm four years younger than William, he always seemed to be my protector. Unlike many big brothers, William never seemed to mind his younger brother hanging around. William had a bicycle, and he would ride me on the handlebars.

We watched professional wrestling on Saturday nights, and we got to where we could do some of the tricks the wrestlers did. He'd show me how to make it look like we were really hurting each other, and when William threw me over his shoulder, he could make it look impressive. A lot of local kids, and even adults liked to watch us wrestle.

William and I were in charge of milking our cows, and one day during the milking, a cow stepped on one of our kittens and killed it. I felt so bad, so William said, 'We'll give the kitten a funeral.' He put it in a cereal box, and we buried it at a nearby gravel pit. William said such a powerful eulogy for that cat, that we both started crying.

Even though William was older than me, I grew up fast, and when I was in the 8th grade, you could barely tell us apart. We looked like twins, so much that I had teachers call me 'William.' We looked very much alike when we were growing up.

People always asked what William would look like without his beard. Well, they can probably look at me and get the answer. I've never had a beard. I went about one week without shaving, and that's as long as I could go.

Growing up on our farm was not easy. We were all expected to work, and work hard. Before and after school, we each had our own chores. We really sweat and labored. William and I would unload a semi full of fertilizer all by ourselves in just a short time. Every job I've ever had was much easier than the work we had to do on the farm. We learned a strong work ethic from the farm that stayed with us all of our lives.

Our dad worked harder than we did, and it took everything he had just to keep our farm going. We had so many tough times. It always seemed that when we finally had a year where we had a beautiful crop, a storm would come through and wipe out half of it.

During our teen years, we picked lots of cotton. But I know for a fact that William didn't pick as much as he says he did! One day, I was in the field and I couldn't find William. Then I looked down at the end of the field, and saw him sitting with three girls, and he was singing to them! He would usually pick just enough cotton to fill up his sack, and then he'd sit on the bag and sing to the local girls who came by.

I think the rock foundation we had came from a praying mother and father. They moaned a lot of prayers for all of us. Even if we don't get to see each other for a few months, William, Lanette and I still have a close bond.

When we were kids, William always protected me, and he has continued to do that over the years. He's tried to guide me, to keep me on the path I needed to stay on.

He stood beside me through thick and thin. When I was broke, he believed in me. He always wanted to see good things happen for his little brother. He's been my mentor and my encourager. William has been the most wonderful brother that I could ever have."

— Ronnie Golden

After getting his fill of farming, Ronnie went into the trucking business. Then he got into cattle and ended up with one of the biggest cattle operations in Florida, as he shipped 100,000 head each year. When cattle prices tanked in 1974, he started selling cars and eventually opened a number of car dealerships.

Ronnie mentioned our backyard wrestling. I think I helped make him pretty tough as we were growing up, and Ronnie went on to be a heck of a football player. He was All-State two years in a row, during his junior and senior years.

When I wasn't wrestling with my brother, I was singing with my sister. Lanette and I sang at any local event that asked us, and a few that didn't. When we weren't singing ourselves, we were going to watch other people perform. We loved attending the all-night gospel sings in Brewton. The Statesman, The Blackwood Brothers and Jake Hess, were our favorites. Some of the events were so large, they had to be held on the football field.

I loved listening to people sing, and during one of those events, we met the Lowery family. They were brothers and sisters who were good singers, and they had an electric guitar player named Rayford. Ray was really good and could play like Chet Atkins and Merle Travis. Lanette and Rayford hit it off, and they eventually married. When she graduated high school, Lanette worked as a bank teller and she traded her dreams of a musical career for a life as a homemaker.

Lanette has always been so prim and proper and very straight-laced, so I have to share a story of the day she out-ran the cops. She was driving our dad's Pontiac, while Ronnie and I were in the backseat. One of Lanette's girlfriends was in the passenger seat as Lanette drove through downtown Brewton. As we all talked, Lanette didn't notice that she was going well over the speed limit...until a police car turned on its lights right behind us.

For some reason, Lanette totally panicked. She pushed the gas pedal to the floor and we took off. From the backseat, I encouraged her with, "He can't arrest you if you get to the state line." We were flying as Lanette came to a narrow one-way bridge. She was able to cross it just before we met another car coming right toward us. The police car had to stop and wait at the bridge and we made it to the Florida border, which was just a couple miles out of town. We all thought we had gotten away with it, but a few days later, Daddy came home and announced, "I was at the barbershop and they were saying William was in my car and he ran from the cops." Lanette calmly said, "Well, I don't believe that."

My sister could drive like Richard Petty, but I did most of my driving on our tractor. I'd go up and down the fields all day long. I grew up in those fields and worked them from the time I was a kid. The roar of the tractor engine was so loud that I found I could sing out, at the top of my lungs, and no one could hear me.

As I sang, I began to daydream. I began to dream big…real big. I could picture in my mind that I was singing in front of thousands of people. I wanted to be performing in front of a bigger crowd than the one that came out for the local peanut boil.

My first introduction to the gospel blues came when I was in the cotton fields. I would listen intently as the older workers sang as they picked the cotton. Their singing helped pass the time, and gave some background music to the many thoughts, plans and dreams that were going through my head. I could actually see a vision for my life. I saw my future, and I was ready to do everything I could to make my visions come true.

I started to get more serious about my singing when I joined our school's FFA quartet. I sang tenor and was singing quite high at the time. Bud Morris was our baritone, Gladden Graves was our lead, and O'Neal Dawson sang bass. O'Neal was really great, and we had a girl who played piano for us. Maxine McKissick was a good player. The other guys had been singing in the quartet for a year before I joined, but they were impressed by my voice and I did have a pretty wide range.

The other guys in the group would come out to our house to rehearse, and our hard work paid off when we competed against other schools. In 1956, when I was a junior in high school, our quartet won the district finals. Our quartet also performed at high school assemblies and a few different events. The FFA quartet is where I first got into four-part harmony. Almost from the instant I heard it, I knew that I had found my calling. I felt that this was what I was supposed to do with my life.

That feeling grew even stronger when I discovered a guy named Elvis. When I saw the impact that Elvis Presley was having on his audiences, I said, "This is what I want to do." When rock and roll hit, I started listening to Chuck Berry, Little Richard and Fats Domino. I always loved rock and roll music, and I liked country music too. I listened to Eddy Arnold and Jim Reeves, and when the bluegrass duo Jim and Jesse came to our high school to perform, I was in the audience.

But Elvis' music really excited me. At the time, my hair was dark black, and I tried to comb it just like Elvis'. I sang "Hound Dog" in the high school talent show, and at another event, I played my guitar as I sang, "Don't Be Cruel."

My singing career was just getting started, but another resident of my hometown had already made it big. Hank Locklin was known for hits like "Please Help Me, I'm Fallin'" and "Send Me the Pillow You Dream On." Hank also became a member of the Grand Ole Opry in 1960. Hank was a star when I was in high school and when he came back home, driving a big, fancy car, he looked like a star.

Hank lived in Brewton until his death in 2009, at the age of 91. He was always very nice to me. Today, when you drive into

Brewton, Alabama, you'll see the large sign that says, "Home of Country Music Legends William Lee Golden of The Oak Ridge Boys and Hank Locklin." Hank Locklin was an inspiration to me. I knew that if a guy from our little town could make it big, then I could too.

FROGENE

I might not have been the smartest boy in our high school…far from it, but I did enjoy my school days. Most of my enjoyment came from singing with the FFA quartet and playing football. After practice, I would bring my football buddies to our house and mother would make biscuits for them.

But the true highlight of my high school years came when I met a girl with the very unique name of Frogene Normand.

Yes, Frogene was her real name. She was named after her father's mother, her grandmother, whose name was Frogene. Her other grandmother was named Rosa, so her mother named her Rosa Frogene. In all my travels, and the thousands of people I've met over the years, I've never met anyone else who had the name Frogene.

Frogene had just moved to Brewton and was named secretary of our senior class. Her family was French, and they spoke French. Her dad worked as a deep-sea diver in Mobile, Alabama, and he had to work almost all the time just to support and feed his 8 children. Frogene had 3 brothers and 4 sisters, and all of them were very musical, especially her brothers.

Frogene's brothers were great singers and musicians. They had a great blend and could harmonize as they sang pop songs like those by The Diamonds, The Ink Spots and The Mills Brothers. Her brothers were members of the FFA quartet before I joined. I saw them sing at a school assembly and I thought they were good enough to "go pro." They were the best singers I had ever heard.

I loved her brother's singing. But I loved Frogene even more. We fell in love very fast and were instant high school sweethearts. We quickly became the king and queen of Brewton. I was voted "Most Popular" and Frogene was named "Most Attractive," and once we joined forces, we seemed to take over our school.

In June of 2020, Frogene knew she was dying of cancer. She knew she had just a couple weeks left to live. But she agreed to sit down for an extended, multi-hour interview for this book. It was a wonderful last gift that she gave to me. During that visit, she laughed and cried as she shared memories that I had long forgotten. Here are a few of those:

> "I met William when I was in the 10th grade. I won't ever forget the first time I saw him. He was standing with some other guys and they were checking out the new crop of girls. William had gone to that school all his life, but I had just moved in and was new to the school. I saw William and his beautiful head of hair. His hair was coal black, and he was very handsome and had a beautiful smile. I thought, 'He is the most perfect man I have ever seen.' He still is, to me…even after all these years, and after his black hair has now turned gray.
>
> Just a few weeks after we started school in September, we had a harvest festival, that included a "Sadie Hawkins" dance, where the girls invited the boys to the dance. I invited William. I wanted to dress as an Indian princess, so I went down to the barn and got some burlap bags that I turned into a dress. William dressed up as Elvis.
>
> Most of our dates were spent at gospel concerts. William's sister was already married, and we would

double date with her and her husband. My parents trusted me and William, as long as Lanette and her husband were along. My parents didn't have much to fear as our average date started when they picked me up after church. We'd have lunch and then go to an afternoon and evening gospel concert. Some of the gospel shows were held at our high school, and they would pack the gymnasium with fans. William started following some of the gospel groups and along the way we saw one that he just fell in love with. Their name was The Oak Ridge Boys.

It's funny the things you start to remember when you start coming up with memories for a book. I remember red clay all over William's car. The road leading to my family's home was red clay. It was like red mud, and no matter how slow you drove, it got all over your tires and then splattered all over the car. William would bring me home from a date, and he'd ask my parents if he could use some water to wash his father's car. He knew he'd get in trouble if that car was covered in red clay.

When William and I first fell in love, there was nothing that could keep us apart. Since his parents only had one car, he always had to get their permission to use it. We had planned a date, but Papa told William, 'One of our best friends has died and we need to drive to the wake.' But William just looked at him and said, 'I need that car tonight. You and Mom have already had your time in life. It's my time now.' As I look back at his line, 'You have already had your time in life,' I have to laugh…Papa and Mama were only 40 years old!

Once we became a couple, William and I thought about little else. That occasionally led to some absentmindedness on William's part. One night, he was supposed to pick up his brother Ronnie after a football game. Ronnie was in the 8th grade, and he waited and waited at the school, but William never showed up. By the time Ronnie finally gave up, everyone else had left the game and the school, so he started walking home...which was 7 miles away. William was with me the entire time, and he had completely forgotten about his little brother. Luckily for him and for Ronnie, a neighbor saw Ronnie as he was driving by, and they stopped and offered him a ride home.

One of my teachers told me that I should not hang around William. They said he was too rowdy and was going to get me in trouble. They basically told me that I was too good for William. I thanked them for their advice, but I didn't agree with them.

From the moment I met him, I had just one life dream...to marry William Lee and have babies. I didn't have any other dream. So, I guess I can say all of my dreams came true."

— Frogene

Frogene and I were so in love, and my family was so poor, that we decided to save money and share one high school yearbook. Frogene ordered a senior annual and told me that I could just share hers. When we got the yearbook, she laughed when we read my senior quote that was next to my photo. It said, "What's Elvis got that I ain't got?" Then Frogene asked me to sign her (our) yearbook. I wrote, "To Frogene, a real friend to the end. William Golden." Yes, I was quite the romantic.

A short time after Frogene passed away, I read that sentence I wrote to her in our yearbook. It might not have been very romantic, but it sure turned out to be true. We were real friends...to the end.

While Frogene excelled in school, I did not. As my senior year went on, I started to get in trouble for skipping class.

Instead of heading to school, I would head to the beach. Brewton was only 35 miles from the Gulf Shores beaches. We were so close to the Gulf Shore Island National Sea Shore, and I thought they were the prettiest beaches in the world. I was fascinated by the beautiful sand dunes that had been created over time.

After football season had ended, I would sometime just get so bored in class, that I would get up and walk out, and never come back for the day. I would sometimes take two or three classmates with me. While the beach was my favorite getaway, one time, I even went to the Mardi Gras in Mobile.

After one of the teachers turned me in for playing hooky, I was called to the principal's office. The principal just happened to be the son of the school superintendent. It was a meeting that would impact my entire life. And it did not go well.

The principal started off understandably with, "If you don't straighten up, I have no problem failing you. And if you don't attend every class, you are going to be expelled." But then he crossed the line, as he stupidly said, "And if you aren't careful, you are going to end up out there on the farm…just like your daddy."

To me, that was a great insult. An insult to me and my father. I stood up to where I looked the principal right in the eyes, as I said, "You don't have to expel me. If that's the way you feel, I don't want to be in this school." And then I really told him what I thought, "I don't know if you know this, but my daddy drives a nicer car than you do. And if a piece of paper diploma makes me an asshole like you, then I don't want one."

As I walked out the door, I stopped and added, "Oh, by the way, my father said if your dad wasn't the superintendent, you wouldn't even have a job."

The principal didn't say a word, and I didn't look back. That was the day I really started learning. I have learned something every day of my life. I have never stopped learning.

I didn't get to graduate with my class, but I did go to summer school and was able to get my diploma. But before that, I got something else…married.

The worst thing about me leaving school, was it meant that I didn't get to see Frogene. She was my first real love and my first girlfriend. Her family lived on one side of town, about 10 miles out of Brewton, while I lived on the opposite side, about 7 miles out of town. That 17 miles doesn't seem like a lot today, but back then, to teenagers who didn't have vehicles, it was like being in another state.

When we were able to get together for our next date, I asked Frogene to marry me. When I thank God for a few of the wise decisions I have made in my life, that is one that tops the list. It was one of the best moves I ever made.

We got married in February of Frogene's senior year of high school. I was 18. She was 17, but just a few months younger than I was. Our wedding day was Feb. 16, 1957, and our ceremony was held at my mom and dad's house. Back then, it was a common thing for people to get married at home. By the way, for anyone wondering…no, we did not "have to" get married. It would be a couple years before our first child was born.

The Monday after our weekend wedding, my new bride…went back to high school. The only real difference came when she got out of school. Instead of going home to her parents, she came home to my parents! We lived with my mother and father, and younger brother Ronnie for the first 6 months of our marriage. Luckily, my sister had moved out when she got married (a unique concept), so her old bedroom became the new home of Mr. and Mrs. William Lee Golden.

Six months later, we moved into a home my uncle had built next door to my grandma and grandpa. The house turned out to be too small for my uncle's family, but it was perfect for the two of us. We fell in love with it and purchased it as our first home.

For the next two years, I farmed and worked for my father, and after she graduated high school, Frogene took a job at the Philip May Company in Brewton. She worked there for ten years. We were a happy couple who loved being together and we had a great time throughout our marriage.

We were both so young when we were newlyweds, and Frogene looked even younger than her 18 years. That played a role in a funny incident that happened when we went camping with another married couple. We were all in a small tent, and in the middle of the night, we started getting eaten up by mosquitos. It got so bad that we all got in our car, so we could sleep.

Frogene and the other girl fell asleep in the backseat and me and the other man slept up front. Before the sun came up, I was woken up by a policeman who was knocking on the window with his flashlight. He asked for our identification, and I groggily replied, "Well, we're all married."

But the cop didn't believe me. He shined his flashlight in the faces of the girls in the back. Then I said, "If we weren't married, do you think we'd be sitting like this?" I pointed at Frogene and added, "I'd be in the back seat with that girl...if I was single."

I put in a full day of work for my father on the farm, but I spent all my free time trying to get my dream of a singing career off the ground. In addition to the time I spent singing as I drove my tractor, I also sang in the shower and continued to sing with my sister, and also with some of Frogene's family.

I tried to put together a group of my own, but I could never get anyone else as interested in it as I was. I tried to find guys who really wanted to sing, but I would get frustrated when I'd book an event and the other guys had other things to do. I'd find a couple new guys who could sing, and we'd perform at a few local events, and then the guys would quit.

I couldn't keep a group together and couldn't get anyone to commit to it like I wanted to. I wanted to stick with it until we made it to "the big time." But it seemed that no one around Brewton believed that we could make a living by singing and playing music. I tried to share my dreams and goals with people, and they would just stare at me and think, "This guy has lost it."

But as I continued pushing ahead, the requests for me to sing started to increase. I began to spend any extra money I had on sound equipment, microphones and speakers. As I began to travel to some dates that were farther from Brewton, I also had to spend money to keep up our car.

Luckily, I had an understanding wife, who believed in me…and my dream. She always had faith in me, and she thought I could do anything that I dreamed I could do. I did too. But when you have a partner who also believes that…there is almost no way you can fail. In the early and very lean days, Frogene sometimes had more faith in me than I did. When my self-confidence turned to doubt, she boosted me up with, "You can do it!" I really don't think I'd be here today without her encouragement of me way back then.

Frogene supported my singing, and none of the great success I would later have, came as a surprise to her. She usually got mad when I wasn't going even further.

With music being such a big part of her family and of course, mine, I knew if we had kids, they would be raised around music. That music would start with lullabies just a short time later.

We were married two years before our first son Rusty came along. Frogene and I were both excited as her due date neared. She felt that she was put on this earth to be a mother, so she couldn't wait. I was a little more nervous, as I wondered how I was going to pay the bills that come with a new baby.

But while I was in the waiting room, waiting for Rusty to be born, I met another soon-to-be father. He was an electrician at the new Container paper mill in Brewton, and he told me I should try to get a job there. Just after I welcomed my new son to the world on January 3rd, I went straight to the papermill and applied for a job.

So, I kicked off 1959 in a big way, with a new baby boy and a new job. The papermill was one of the better jobs in Brewton, depending on what your position was in the factory. I was a utility man there and it was probably the worst job at the plant. Wherever there was trouble or problems, that's where I was sent.

I eventually moved to the recovery area, which was a very dangerous job, where I had to work with caustic chemicals. It was made to break down and dissolve wood chips. The chips went into huge 4 story tall silos, and we put the chemicals in, added steam to it, and turned the wood into mush.

On my first day, I was warned that if I fell into the fiery cauldron of toxin, my body would completely dissolve into nothing in just a few seconds. If you got any of those poisonous chemicals on your clothes, it would destroy them instantly.

I also had to pour hot, melted smelt into huge vat drums of even hotter liquid. It exploded as it hit, and I was working right on top of all of that. I'd keep pouring, and I'd have to keep it from clogging up. I wore a face mask, because it would pop out and get on your skin. When it landed on your arm, it would leave a scar. That burnt lime was bad.

In addition to the danger, the mill also smelled horrible. After being in the middle of it for eight hours a day, the odor would seep into my skin. When I'd get off work and pull into our driveway, my wife would make me take my clothes off before I came inside the house. I'd just laugh and say, "That's the smell of money."

Can you believe that's the dirty and dangerous job I had when the Oak Ridge Boys offered me the chance to join their group? It's true. But I'll get to that in just a bit.

Frogene and I spent most of our free time going to concerts. We traveled to Memphis for a weekend to attend the Quartet Convention at Ellis Auditorium. We sat in the nosebleed seats, but we were happy just to be in the building, to see our favorite group…yes, The Oak Ridge Boys.

When we got back from the Quartet Convention, I returned to the papermill. But during my breaks, I would get a stack of paper towels, and I'd sit and write my name on each one. I practiced signing my autograph until I found the one I thought was perfect. It was a flowing, very readable signature. I could vision the day someone would ask for my autograph. When that day came, I wanted them to be able to read every letter of my name.

I practiced my autograph as I worked at the papermill for almost six years. I started there just after my first son was born. I was there two years later, when our second son Craig was born, and two years later, when we welcomed our third son Chris, I was still at the mill.

Since our home was pretty small, when our boys were little, they all slept in the same room. My nephew Ron also stayed with us quite a bit, and he was also in the same room. We had two queen size beds and the four boys slept in those two beds. As boys can do, most nights, they would talk and laugh until I yelled at them and told them to go to sleep.

Frogene loved every minute of raising our boys. She was very happy and content being my wife and being a mother. She was always happiest when all her sons were with her. As they grew up, I found that our boys were all different. They were each their own individual. I used to say, "I've got 3 sons...one of each."

As I continued to work at the mill, I also continued to work toward the vision I saw for my life. I was not a papermill worker who sang. I was a singer, who happened to work at a papermill...at least for a little while longer.

I continued to sing with some guys around town. One was a doctor who invited me to sing with his barbershop group. I didn't know much about that kind of singing, and I was not used to singing acapella with just a pitch pipe. Ironically, many decades later, the Oak Ridge Boys have used only a pitch pipe as we sang acapella numerous times. Most of those were at funerals or when we sang the National Anthem.

I enjoyed the barbershop group, but my heart was in gospel and country music. After some more searching, I finally found a couple of young men who would help me get a little closer to my big goal. I formed a group I called The Pilots Trio. Randy McDaniel and his nephew Hack McCluskey were the other two "Pilots." They lived in Jay, Florida, so after working in the papermill, I would drive to Florida, so we could rehearse. My first "big" television appearance came with The Pilots Trio. It was on a country music TV show that was taped in Jacksonville, Florida. It aired all over the state of Florida and it instantly boosted the bookings for our live concerts. It was the first time that I saw the power of television.

While our group was based out of Jay, Florida, we always told everyone we were from Pensacola. We did that because we thought Pensacola sounded more impressive. I came up with the "Pilots" name to play up on the Blue Angels, who were from Pensacola.

One of the first people to promote and book some of our Pilot Trio shows was J.G. Whitfield. J.G. was a bass singer who had helped start the Florida Boys and Dixie Echoes, and he also promoted concerts. J.G. had gone to school with my mom and dad. His wife owned a big grocery store, and she sponsored his radio show. He did that show from the middle of the store, and he played gospel music while he promoted all the grocery specials. J.G. went on to become a big promoter, and he booked a lot of gospel shows for the Oak Ridge Boys.

As our Pilots Trio group grew in popularity, we were asked to take part in a number of "All-Night Singings" in Mobile and Pensacola. Those big events would feature a lot of different acts, and I was so excited when I saw the name The Oak Ridge Boys at the top of the show bill.

In 1962, the Oaks put out two albums with Gary McSpadden singing lead. Those two albums really turned me on to what the Oak Ridge Boys were doing in gospel music. One was called "The Sounds of Nashville," and it really had a country music type feel, as you would guess from the title. The other album was titled "Folk Minded Spirituals for Spiritual Minded Folks."

I was a big fan of Gary McSpadden. When he joined the group, I thought he helped them become cutting edge and innovative. In my opinion, the early Oaks were at their very best when Gary McSpadden was with them.

During an all-night sing concert in Bonifay, Florida, I visited with Gary and the other Oak Ridge Boys before my Pilots Trio did our portion of the show. After the concert, as they signed autographs at their record rack, they told me that they were impressed with what they saw and heard in my singing.

We did a number of similar concerts together and our paths continued to cross as The Oaks and The Pilots Trio played the southern gospel circuit. And I had a feeling that my career was finally about ready for take-off.

A DREAM COMES TRUE

In 1964, I joined the group that I would be with for the rest of my life. I've been with them for more than 55 years. That group is…the Masons.

I joined the Masonic Lodge when I was 23 years old, and I became a Master Mason the year before I joined the Oaks. I eventually went on to become a third-degree Mason. Rex Wiseman, who plays with the Oak Ridge Boys, is also a Mason, and his father and brothers are all Masons. I was not able to attend lodge meetings, because I was always on the road, but I've always stayed in good standing as a Mason.

A few years ago, I also became a Shriner. I went through the process at the temple in Nashville. The Masons and Shriners have blessed my life. But the true calling of my life would come a year after I joined the Masons.

Life is about finding your passions, and then following those. I felt led to pursue what my visions were. That's when you find total fulfillment. In your life, there are certain things you have to do in order to reach your dreams and goals. For me, I knew that staying in Brewton and working at the papermill was not where I wanted to be. I also knew that no one was going to come to me to make my dreams come true. I had to go to them.

My biggest dream was to be an Oak Ridge Boy. They were my favorite group. The Oaks were young guys who had a more modern type of gospel music, and I thought they were great.

When Gary McSpadden left the group, to go with Jake Hess to make The Imperials, it just made me sick. Gary was replaced by Jim Hammill, and I didn't think Jim fit in at all with the group. I was so upset with the change to my favorite group, that I decided to drive to Nashville to tell them what I thought. While I was there, I would also tell them who I thought could help them get back to where they needed to be…me.

When I got to the church where the Oaks were playing, I met with Smitty Gatlin, who was the lead singer of the group. I was very honest with Smitty, as I gave him my opinion of the current Oaks, and I told him if they ever needed a baritone singer, that I would love to try out for the position. Smitty said they didn't have an opening at the time, but he called Ben Speers, and asked if The Speers would audition me for an opening with their group. I think he was really wanting to use Ben to see what I could do!

Ben gave me shape notes music to read. I told him I couldn't read music, and Ben said all their group had to read music. (I still can't read music today.) I'm so thankful I didn't get a job with The Speers. That is not where my heart was. I really only had my heart set on one group…the Oak Ridge Boys.

Two months after my meeting with Smitty, I was back working at the Brewton paper mill and still singing on the weekends with my group The Pilots Trio. That's what I was doing when I got the call that changed my life. When I said hello, Smitty Gatlin said, "William, Jim Hammill is leaving us, and we were wondering if you were still interested in trying out for a job with us." I'm sure he could hear me smiling through the phone as I said, "Yes, I am."

I came up to Nashville the next week and tried out. After I sang a couple songs for them, Smitty asked, "When can you start?" I replied, "When do you need me?" He said, "Next week."

I headed back to Brewton to turn in my resignation at the papermill. My dream and vision had come true. I was going to be an Oak Ridge Boy. As I neared my hometown, memories of my years driving a tractor on the farm flooded my mind. Back when I was on that tractor, I could see everything. I would share my vision and dreams and goals with other people, and it was like I was talking to a fence post. They couldn't see it. They thought I was pipe dreaming.

One of those who thought I was crazy, was my dad. When I told him I had just been hired by the Oak Ridge Boys, and that I was giving up my job at the papermill, daddy was totally against it. Dad didn't want me moving to "the big city." And six months later, his objection would turn to total heartache when I broke the news that our entire family, including dad's 3 grandsons would be moving to Nashville.

I joined the Oaks in January of 1965. Frogene and I decided to keep our boys in Brewton through the end of the school year, but they would all join me in Music City that summer. Until then, once a month, I would get a break from the road and I'd run back down to Brewton for 2 or 3 days. If the Oaks came back to Nashville for just a day or two, I didn't have time to go be with my family, so I'd just stay in a cheap motel in Nashville or I would sleep on the bus. I missed being with my family, but when I did get back home, we made the most of it, and we cherished the time we had together.

When our entire family moved to Nashville, it was hard on my mom and dad. For the rest of his life, my father never gave up hope that we would move back to Brewton. Every single time, when we would go back for Christmas or some other occasion, our visit always ended the same way…as we walked to the car, dad would beg me, "Son, when are you going to come back home to stay? I wish you would raise your family here." I always gave dad the same answer, "When I'm done singing with the Oaks, when I've done everything I have to do there, I will move back to the farm. I promise."

But we also brought a little bit of the farm with us when we moved to the big city. My brother Ronnie helped move all our belongings, but there would be no fancy U-Haul truck for us. Instead, Ronnie washed out an old cattle trailer. He used a firehose to clean it real good, and we loaded all our furniture in it. We probably looked a little like the Beverly Hillbillies, and when we passed the Nashville city limit sign, I yelled, "Well, country has come to town!"

As soon as I left Brewton, I focused all my attention on making the Oak Ridge Boys the biggest act I possibly could. The main lineup for the 1965 Oak Ridge Boys included Smitty Gatlin, Herman Harper, Little Willie Wynn, myself, and Tommy Fairchild was our piano player. At the time, Little Willie was probably the most popular guy in the group. People always ask how he got the name "Little Willie." It's pretty simple. When he joined the Oaks at the age of 21, he weighed just 119 pounds, so they started calling him Little Willie.

Willie and I are the only two still around from the original group when I joined them. Willie is a year older than me. As I was writing this chapter, I called him and asked him to share a few memories of our time together:

> "William used to come to our concerts when he was a teenager. But a few years later, he was up on stage, singing with us. Bill (I always called him Bill, and still do) wanted to be a star, and he went after his dreams with a drive that I've never seen in anyone else. He worked as hard as he could to reach his goals. I don't think there's ever been a human being who wanted 'to make it' as much as he did.
>
> We both had a lot in common. Bill was a good ol' farm boy from south Alabama and I was a farm boy from south

Georgia. But once he started entertaining, he didn't look like a farm boy. He looked like a star. He looked like a magazine model. When we were on the road, before we went on stage, we would sometimes have to wait for Bill to get every hair in place. He made sure that his hair was just perfect. And he also kept the rest of us looking good too. He cut all our hair. He was better than any barber.

The Oak Ridge Boys were hotter than a pistol and people would give us a standing ovation as soon as we came out. In gospel music, we were as popular as you could get. And we did everything we could to stay popular. Those boys worked their tails off. And when the group switched to country music, the Oaks continued to work harder than everyone else.

Bill has a great sense of humor. Golden used to be the practical joker of the group. He told funny stories and kept us laughing as we'd ride down the road. Bill is a true star, and he was the most energetic guy you ever saw in your life.

I love all the Oak Ridge Boys. In my opinion, they will always be the best group out there. Bill and I are still very close, and even though I left the group in 1973, I stayed close with Bill. He has a heart of gold, and he's my buddy."

— Little Willie Wynn

I love Little Willie. But I can't sing like him. Smitty asked me to go to a voice teacher, whose name was Miss Manley. She had taught Little Willie Wynn his high, nasal singing technique and she thought I should also sing through my nose. I tried to sing that way on the classic song, "Danny Boy," and before it was over, I knew I was wasting my time.

I went to another vocal teacher, Mr. Drummond, who thought I should use a completely different approach. He instructed me how to sing in a big operatic voice. By the time the two voice teachers got done with me, I was totally screwed up and quite confused. For the first time, I even questioned whether I should be singing at all. I found myself almost scared to sing. I had lost all the self-confidence that had helped bring me to Nashville. But I finally told myself, "I am not an opera singer, and I don't sing through my nose. I sing from my soul. I need to just be myself."

When I first joined the Oaks, each member had a job to do. My job was to help lug in all the sound equipment. I was our roadie. I had to set up all the speakers, sound board and microphones, and then I'd go backstage, change clothes and get ready to go out and sing.

After the show, we'd go out to the record rack where we autographed our latest album. Signing autographs and meeting the fans allowed us to get the fans' immediate response to what we were doing. The fans would come up and tell us what songs they liked and which ones they didn't. The "merch table" and "record rack" were also where we made a lot of our money. We sold song books, pictures and records…lots of records. When we left on a long tour, we got to where we would pack up to 15, 000 record albums under the bus.

If you happen to have a photo that you took of me signing one of the albums back then, I can guarantee you that it will show me smiling ear to ear. I was doing something that I loved to do, with the group that I loved. I had looked up to them and was a fan of their music, and now I was one of them! It was a dream come true.

The first album I did with the Oak Ridge Boys had a kind of bluegrass feel. The Starday Records album had the very humble title of, "The Sensational Oak Ridge Boys from Nashville, Tennessee." For the cover shot, we all stood in front of a log cabin that was located off Granny White Pike in Nashville. Just before our photo shoot, I went to the Nashville Shirt Shop and bought us all brand new, identical shirts. Each guy gave me their size and they trusted me to pick out something good for us. They were cheap shirts, but they sure looked good. We wore those shirts until there was almost nothing left of them.

My second album with the group was titled "International." We took a photo for the cover photo that looked like we were way out in Arizona, but we were actually just off the intersection of I-40 and I-24 in Nashville.

Even though he had left the group before I joined, I became friends with Gary McSpadden right after I joined the Oaks. I lived a half mile from him, and I'd see him or his wife at the store or gas station. We became friends, and our wives became close friends. Gary was into photography and he asked if he could take my photo. Gary took most of the promotional photos of the Oak Ridge Boys during that time.

In January of '65, we played a big show at the Will Rogers Memorial Auditorium in Fort Worth, Texas. The Statesmen, The Blackwoods and The Speer Family were also on the show. In the audience that night was a young man named Duane Allen. Duane introduced himself to me in the hallway. A year and a half later I would be introducing him on stage as our newest Oak Ridge Boy.

FOUR OAKS

In October of '65, the Oak Ridge Boys became one of the first gospel acts to have an outside manager, as Don Light signed us to his new Gospel Music Talent Agency. Don had his own radio show and then he wound up working as a Billboard reporter. He went to all the shows and got to know the inside of the business, from the managers, agents, record labels to PR people.

Don also started the Gospel Music Association, which he patterned it after the Country Music Association, and he helped bring gospel music to a much more professional level. Don took over our bookings and used official and binding contracts, (Something that was almost unheard of when acts were booked by different churches.)

The Oak Ridge Boys and the Happy Goodman Family were the first two acts to join Don's agency. We knew we were in high cotton as the fairly new Happy Goodman Family had just blown the gospel music scene out of the water. They became the hottest thing around and sold out every arena they played. They had an old-time gospel sound, but they came with such an energy that just electrified peoplc.

As our bookings increased under Don Light's management, we began to travel almost constantly. To pass the time on the road, our favorite pastime was playing practical jokes on other gospel groups or members of our own group. Some jokes were simple like the night we found a stray dog off the street and put it in Little Willie Wynn's bunk on the bus.

Others were more elaborate, like one night when we opened for the Speer Family. Before we got to the venue, we stopped at a bait shop and purchased some crickets. While the Speer Family was performing on stage, we dumped the crickets into the bus. We headed out of town before the Speers got back to their very noisy bus. One cricket would drive you crazy, but a bus full is pretty cruel.

Crickets are loud, but at least they don't stink. We once limburger cheesed the Happy Goodman Family. We opened the show and when they took to the stage, we took a bunch of limburger cheese and put it in the air vents of their bus. We put some under the bus, too.

Many years later, I did the same thing to Michael Sykes when he was recording in the studio. He had been producing an Oak Ridge Boys session, and on our last day of recording, as we got ready to leave, I put limburger cheese in a few different spots, all around the building. I put some down in the bathtub drain, and some under the kitchen sink. I wanted it in different locations so when they would find one, they would think that would solve the problem. But they were everywhere!

A few days later, I went back to the studio, and Michael had more than a dozen scented candles burning. As soon as I walked in, he said "Bill Gaither was doing a big recording here yesterday and it smelled so bad." I just smiled as Michael continued, "I think there's a dead rat inside a wall. I've been spraying air freshener, but it just keeps getting worse and worse, and nothing helps."

That cheese was festering real good by the time Gaither got there. I finally fessed up that I was the one who did it, and I think that Michael has finally forgiven me. But he'll never eat limburger cheese again.

In my very early days with the group, we once pushed a guy out of the bus. We had an old Greyhound bus that Greyhound had already worn out. To say that the bus' plumbing system was a little outdated would be an understatement. We didn't have an actual bathroom on the bus. Even when we did get one, you were not allowed to do "number 2" on the bus. That was a given. You waited until we came to a gas station or at least a heavily wooded area.

But we could urinate…through a state-of-the-art funnel that was attached to a hose that ran outside the bus. The funnel was up front, near the door, at the bottom of the steps. When you stood there, you could use the bathroom and no one on the bus could see you. Ah, the glamorous life of the stars!

One night, the bus was parked, and Herman Harper got up and went up front to use the bathroom. He was in his underwear and as he urinated, someone snuck up to the driver's seat, pulled the handle of the door and pushed Herman out. Before he could step back in, the bus pulled away. Herman was standing there in his underwear on the square of a small Georgia town. We drove about a mile and then turned around and came back to get him.

While I was spending all my time in a bus, my wife was too. At home in Hendersonville, Frogene came up with an idea of buying her own school bus. I thought she was crazy, but after she explained her request, I went with her to pick out a good one.

When Frogene took our boys to Good Pasture School, she saw a lot of students who had to walk long distances, or whose parents had to bring them to school and then pick them up. Frogene got all their names and then asked their parents, "If I buy a bus, would you pay me a dollar a day to take your child to school?"

Everyone said "Yes," and for the next 9 years, my wife was a school bus driver, in a bus she owned.

When they had school field trips or the teams needed to get to a ballgame, the school started hiring her. Frogene loved driving a bus and she used the money she made from that to put our sons through private school. She was making more in her school bus than I was in our Oak Ridge Boys' tour bus!

I had been with the group for about a year, when the Oaks did a show in Huntington, West Virginia. Our opening act was a group called The Prophets. Duane Allen was now a part of that act. Smitty Gatlin was planning to leave the Oaks, so we talked to Duane about him possibly joining our group. Duane told us that he had loved the Oak Ridge Boys since the late 1950s. He explained how he had dreamed of being an Oak Ridge Boy, since he was little, but he had just been drafted and was headed to the Army.

On April 30, 1966, Duane went to Paris, Texas, where he planned to be inducted into the U.S. Army, but at the last second, he received a medical discharge due to a heart condition. The day after Duane's discharge, the Oak Ridge Boys met in Nashville to discuss our next move. Smitty wanted to get off the road and he had just left the group. Little Willie, Herman Harper and I talked about possible replacements for Smitty, and we all kept coming back to one name…Duane Allen.

Duane was our first and basically only choice. When we had met him, he had been so enthusiastic, as he told how he had all our albums and already knew all our songs. But we knew we couldn't fight the Army, and I figured Duane was probably already halfway to Vietnam.

But during a meeting at our manager, Don Light's office, Herman Harper asked Don's secretary to try to call Duane one last time. At the exact moment she was dialing the phone, the door opened and Duane Allen walked in. We were all flabbergasted. Herman Harper asked him, "What are you doin' here?" Duane laughed, "I'm lookin' for a job." Duane explained that as soon as they had discharged him, he had driven all night from Texas to Nashville. His timing couldn't have been better. It had to be a God thing.

We took him over to a little church on Trinity Lane, and we sang two songs together. That was the day Duane Allen became an Oak Ridge Boy. I was for Duane all the way, and I thought he was perfect for the group. He has a trained voice, and he studied voice and music in college. He was a young guy and he already had that great, big voice that we needed in gospel music.

Smitty Gatlin was a hard act to follow. People loved him. They loved his singing and his sense of humor. But Duane Allen was more than up to making people forget Smitty. In addition to singing, Duane did most of our emcee work. During that time, Duane would introduce me as "Bill Golden." I had always gone by William, but when he started calling me Bill, I signed autographs as Bill for a few years, and many people in gospel music knew me as Bill Golden.

But when we went into country music, we were doing a television taping at the Opry house, and someone yelled, "Hey Bill!" I looked around thinking they wanted me, but they were calling someone else. I glanced across the room and saw a bunch of Bills. I saw Bill Carlisle, Billy Walker and Bill Anderson, and right then, I said to myself, "I am going to use the name I was born with." From that point on, I signed my name William Lee Golden.

Just after Duane joined us, we sang on the Grand Ole Opry for the very first time. Bill Anderson put us on his portion of the Opry, and we sang a song he wrote called "Great, Great Day." It was the title song from our latest album. I'll always remember when Duane and I walked up the steps that led to the back door of the Ryman Auditorium. I was in awe as we stood at the side of the stage, waiting to go on. It's hard to believe that Bill

Anderson and the Oak Ridge Boys are still singing on the Opry, more than 50 years later!

A short time after Duane joined the group, Herman Harper left us. He wanted to spend more time with his three young sons, and he was also singing background on the Grand Ole Opry. When Herman left, I was voted in as manager of the group, and my first move was to call Noel Fox, and offer him the job of being our bass singer. Noel was a great one. He was a great singer, who sang with such emotion. He felt that music; it touched him and he touched the audience.

When you travel as much as we have over the years, you'll have your fair share of breakdowns and accidents. Some of those were fairly minor, like the night our tour bus hit a mule as we were driving through Mississippi. On two separate occasions, we hit horses that ran out in front of us. But others were much more serious. Our bus hit a car full of people one night in Louisiana. It was about midnight and I was sitting up front as we barreled down a rural highway. I saw a car sitting on the right hand shoulder, but just as we got up to it, they not only pulled out onto the road, but they made a sharp left turn, to try to cross the road. They turned left, right in front of us and we hit them broadside…twice. The first impact sent the car down the highway, and before the bus came to a stop, we hit them again. It was a miracle that no one lost their life that night. When you get a big tour bus in your ear at 60 miles an hour, things usually don't turn out very good.

In our gospel days, we took turns driving the bus, and I was behind the wheel for one of our worst wrecks: We were passing through Illinois, on our way to Bloomington, Indiana. The night before, the Oaks had done a show with the Speer Family, and both groups were going to follow each other to the Indiana concert. The Speers' bus was ahead of us, as I drove ours. Duane was sitting in the jumpseat, right behind the stairs, next to me.

We were directly behind the Speers on a narrow two- lane road as we crossed a real long, very high bridge. We were meeting a long line of oncoming traffic, and a guy pulled out to pass, and was coming head on toward the Speers' bus. Their driver, O'Neil Terry, slammed on his brakes. He just locked them up. I tried to stop, but the brakes on our older bus weren't that good. I pushed them to the floor, but I knew there was no way I wasn't going to drive right through the back of the Speers' bus. On the middle of that bridge, there was nowhere to go.

I yelled, "Guys, hold on! We're gonna hit 'em." I couldn't pull over into the left lane or we would have hit an oncoming car head on, and if I went to the right, we would have plummeted over the bridge. But I turned the steering wheel just enough to the left, so that the main impact hit the stair area of our bus.

Duane was thrown through our front windshield. His body actually hit the back of the Speers' bus, busted out their back window and then he bounced back into our bus. A second later, a car that was following us, hit us in the back.

When we all finally came to a stop, the back part of the Speer Family bus was sitting in the stair area of our bus. Their bus was 6 feet into ours, and Duane's left arm was in their back lounge. It's a miracle he wasn't killed, but he walked away with only bumps and bruises.

Another person who could have very easily died that day was Little Willie Wynn. Since both groups were headed to the same concert, at the time of the accident, Little Willie was riding on the Speers' bus. He was sitting in the back room, playing rummy with Ben Speers when the crash happened.

The crash took out the right half of our bus, and I know if I hadn't turned a little left, I would have been totally crushed. That other bus would have gone right through me. When Brock

Speer saw all the damage, he yelled to Little Willie, "Willie, hold me!" And he totally fainted and just fell into Willie's arms. Mom Speer was very religious, and she always said that we had that accident because Ben and Little Willie were in the back, playing cards.

A wrecker towed our bus to Chicago, but we somehow managed to get to our concert that night. We were about 3 hours late, and we were picking out glass from Duane's arms, my head and face just before we walked on stage, but we performed…after we gave thanks to God for saving our lives.

With our bus totaled, we planned to rent a station wagon. I went to Fay Sims, a singer and car dealer in Chattanooga, Tennessee to see if he had a vehicle we could rent. Fay loved the Oak Ridge Boys, and he said he would loan us a station wagon for free. We had five members at the time and with all our luggage and equipment, we all had to sleep sitting up. Six months later, I returned the car to Fay, and he was quite surprised at the huge amount of miles we had put on it in just six months!

Back home in Hendersonville, our guest room was filled with a new guest. Her name was Norah Lee. But the man who remembers those days better than I do, is Duane Allen. He should. He married Norah Lee:

"Norah Lee was from Bowling Green, Kentucky, and she took a job at a music publishing company. The first date I had with her, was a double date with Herman Harper and his wife. They took us out to St. Clare's in Nashville to have dinner. Norah Lee stayed with Herman and Jo for a short while, and then she moved in with Frogene and William Lee. The publishing company didn't pay very much, so she stayed with them until she saved up enough money to get a room at another place. When I was dating Norah, I'd go to William's house to pick her

---

up. Frogene and William were great to her and they treated her like family."

— Duane Allen

Not only did we take our gospel music across the country, but also around the world. We toured Sweden and Europe and did concerts in Stockholm and Norway.

During those tours, I got to know the Samuelson Brothers, who were a popular gospel/country act in Sweden. We toured with them in Finland, Denmark and Sweden. The Samuelsons were also with us when we traveled to Russia. Long before we would go behind the Iron Curtain with Roy Clark on a huge country music tour, I booked us to sing contemporary gospel music in Russia.

During our overseas tours, we met a young promoter named Christer Hamrin. He was only 16 years old, but he was very sharp. He booked us on some national radio shows in Scandinavia, and a year later, he booked and promoted concerts for us. When he got older, Christer moved to Los Angeles, and he is still an impressive man.

We had some great times and expanded our horizons as singers and performers, as we traveled in Europe and Norway. Looking back, it's pretty amazing that we toured Europe when we were still a gospel group. Traveling to different countries was fun and very educational. We would usually go over for 10 days or 2 weeks, and go from one country to another. We sang to people who didn't always understand exactly what we were saying or singing, but they were still "getting" us. The response we received during the shows always made us feel so good.

One thing we quickly noticed when we played in those countries, was that we were seeing young people who were getting turned on to what we were doing. Even though we were drawing younger people to gospel music here in the U.S., when we went to Europe, the crowds were even younger. Over there, young people were really into gospel music, and because of our young age, they were attracted to our concerts. Back then, we were the young guys when most of the other gospel acts were older guys. Now, we are the old guys!

Back in the U.S., we opened the concerts for Governor Jimmie Davis and we also sang backup for him during his part of the show. Jimmie Davis had been the governor of the state of Louisiana, but he was also a very popular gospel and country music entertainer. In August of 1967, Governor Davis asked us to sing behind him when he performed his signature song "Suppertime" on "The Tonight Show" with Johnny Carson. That would be the first of many appearances for us on that show.

Tommy Fairchild was our long-time musical arranger and accompanist, but we featured him out front to expand the look of the group from 4 to 5 members. During our gospel years, we had the main 4 singers, but we also included all the band members on our album covers. But we always had just 4 official members.

In the late '60s, we found ourselves playing in a very unique location. We sang in a confederate graveyard, 8 miles outside Many, Louisiana. We had to dress in the nearby woods, and we hung our clothes on a tree limb and tried to hide behind a bush as we put our pants on.

We sang in front of the tomb of the unknown soldier, and once we began our "show", we had only an antique upright piano and one microphone. Since our bass singer's voice couldn't carry as loud as the rest of us, we had to move him in real close to the one mic.

Our cemetery concert came as the Oak Ridge Boys themselves were struggling to survive. We were going through some very lean years. At the end of our concerts, we'd count the money we had made, and a lot of times there was none to count, especially during those "love offerings" that a lot of churches liked to pay us with. It always seemed there was more "love" than "offering" and it was hard to keep our tour bus gassed up when we were paid in "love."

Luckily, the new drummer we introduced in 1968, didn't demand a lot of money. It was my son Rusty…who was just 8 years old! He played a concert with us in Crestview, Florida. It was his first pro gig, and he wasn't very good. Heck, he was only 8. What did we expect? But he could keep a beat, and it got us through the show. Rusty also played a B3 organ and drums for us on a number of occasions.

By the time he was 12, Rusty was such a good drummer that he went out on tour with the gospel group The Rambos. They were huge at the time. When they played the National Quartet Convention, Elvis sat at the side of the stage and watched Rusty drumming behind The Rambos.

The same year that Rusty made his debut with us, I received a letter that boosted my confidence. It was from a woman named Ruby Moore, who asked if she could be our fan club president. I took it as a good sign that even though we were struggling to pay our bills, Ruby thought we were popular enough that we should have our own fan club.

Ruby became our club president, and she sent out newsletters to keep our fans up to date on what the Oaks were doing and where we were playing. A short time later, Kathy Harris took over the fan club duties. Kathy had majored in journalism, and also sang in a gospel group. Believe it or not, Kathy is still with the Oaks' organization today.

In an effort to boost our visibility, I started asking one of the best promoters in Nashville for some advice. Lon Varnell had been promoting big arena shows that included The Harlem Globetrotters and Lawrence Welk's orchestra. Lawrence Welk later told me that he only played concerts that Lon booked and promoted.

Lon Varnell taught me how to get free advertising from newspapers and local television stations. He taught me the importance of running ads in newspapers that did stories on us, and he also taught me about TV and radio advertising. I learned how to promote and more importantly, where and when to promote. There was always something to learn about the business and I never got tired of learning. I learned the different sides of the business, and it was all so exciting to me.

I started putting together all the promotional material for the Oak Ridge Boys, and then I sent it to people who wanted to help promote and book our shows. I paid for photographers to do photo shoots for us and we used the photos to make 8x10s we sold at our concerts. We also used the photos on posters that I would put up around the town we would soon be playing in. Doing the show was the easiest part of my day!

We also found that the more people were able to see what we did, the more people liked us. So, we pooled our money and rented a Nashville television studio where we started videotaping some live performances. To make it more impressive, we'd bring college kids in to be our audience. Those turned out so well, that we took them to Jake Hess and Ron Page who had a TV show in Nashville. They played everything we gave them. Elmer Childress had a similar show in Wichita, Kansas. Elmer played our videos on his Classic Country show on KARD TV.

In the late '60s, I went to see Lee Bryant, who owned KTAL-TV, Channel 6 in Shreveport, Louisiana. Lee had seen us perform on TV, and had contacted me to say he would like to give us our own TV show. Lee really took a personal interest in the group, and in just a short time, "It's Happening with the Oak Ridge Boys" was on the air. Duane Allen has these thoughts about our first television work:

"To pay for the production of 'It's Happening with the Oak Ridge Boys,' we needed a sponsor. So, William and I went to Athens, Alabama to meet with the man who owned 'Sweet Sue Chicken and Dumplins.' I wrote a special jingle for them that I still remember today: 'It will make you jingle, it will make you shout. Sweet Sue Chicken and Dumplins turn my taste buds inside out.' We recorded that in a little studio, and that sold them on sponsoring us. We made a video of us singing the jingle for our TV show, and when our show became syndicated and started airing in other parts of the country, Sweet Sue Chicken agreed to sponsor us in 25 television markets.

As the show's popularity grew, William and I went to Memphis, where we got the Downtowner Hotel chain to also sponsor the show. It didn't hurt that the chain was run by a former bass singer who had been in the Oak Ridge Quartet. He bought another 17 markets. So, we were on television in 42 different parts of the country with those two sponsors. One of those new markets was Denver, Colorado. I flew out to Denver to meet with the different TV stations, hoping that one would give us a timeslot to air our show. I took big video tapes with me, so I could play them for the station managers.

We were so excited to be singing on TV, and that exposure helped us in so many ways. It helped get us new bookings and then when we went to perform in those places where the show aired, our crowds were always much larger.

When I joined the Oak Ridge Boys, I got the job of my dreams. They were always the group I wanted to sing with. And when I think back to Sweet Sue Chicken and Dumplins, I have to laugh, because not a whole lot has changed for us. Today, we are eating Gus Arrendale's

> Springer Mountain Farm Chicken, and dumplins from Cracker Barrel!"
>
> — Duane Allen

Back then, a favorite part of our live show was when we did impressions of other top gospel acts. We did a song called "Go Out to the Program." We imitated 4 or 5 big groups including the Chuck Wagon Gang, The Blackwoods, the Statesmen Quartets, the Happy Goodman Family, and The Speer Family. Little Willie would sing the lady parts and people loved it. The people who loved gospel music knew all those groups, and it was funny. But we also had the talent to sound just like those different groups.

In the late '60s and early '70s, we performed at a lot of schools. In my mementos, I still have a high school newspaper that had us on the front page in 1970. More than 50 years have passed, but I still remember those school assemblies. For the teenagers, we sang songs that were positive, but not necessarily religious. We were usually booked for a concert that evening, (one where we sold tickets), but first we'd come in and sing songs for the students in the afternoon. And every single time we did that, we would have a bigger crowd that night. We knew if we could get the kids excited about our music during the day, they would go home and bring their parents to the show that evening.

We built a younger audience through those schools. The kids who were 16 years old then are now 67 years old, and many of them have been coming to our shows for five decades. It took a little extra time to do a school assembly, but it always paid off.

My experience in concert promotion paid off in 1969, when I came up with the idea of hosting a truly international event. I wanted to bring gospel acts from around the world to Nashville for a 2-day event that I called "The International Gospel Music Festival."

One of the first acts I booked was our friends The Samuelsons, who we met when we toured Sweden. We also had groups from Mexico, Canada and a few other countries. Of course, the Oak Ridge Boys were the host group. I asked my friend J.G. Whitfield to help me book and promote the event, and we ended up becoming partners for the festival.

The festival took place at the Nashville Municipal Auditorium and the event was a big success. More than 10, 000 fans turned out, and we set an attendance record for a gospel music event in Nashville. The festival ran for a few years and attendance grew every year, with an average of 15, 000 people each year.

One of the things that set the Oak Ridge Boys apart from other gospel groups of the '60s and '70s was our band. It was different than anything gospel music had ever seen. I guess you could say we were marching to the beat of a different drum…or in our case, different drummer. In 1969, we hired Mark Ellerbee. Mark was a rock and roll drummer who could really communicate with the young people in our audience. He was a hippie and was so much fun to work with. He had been a medic in Vietnam, but he studied classical music in college. He was a great guy, a great player and everybody loved Mark.

A short time later, Don Breland came aboard as our bass guitar player. Don had worked with the Rambos when he was just a teenager, and he still wasn't even 18 years old when he joined us. Since he was so young, he lived with Duane Allen and his wife. Don became a fan favorite almost instantly.

That year, we won two Gospel Music Association Dove awards, one for Best Gospel Album for "It's Happening," and the other for the "Best Album Cover." A year later, we'd win another Dove as we were named "Group of the Year." Over the next 5 years, we'd win a dozen Dove awards.

In 1970, the Oak Ridge Boys' album "Talk About the Good Times," won our first Grammy Award for Best Gospel Performance. And the group got even better when John Rich joined us in 1972. John was multi-talented and could play acoustic guitar, electric guitar, and steel guitar. John was a key part of our now cutting edge and innovative group. I'm not afraid to say it... we were just a little cooler than the rest of the gospel groups at the time.

As a lot of people did in the early '70s, we started growing our hair longer. And while our appearance was changing, so was our music. We started doing more secular type songs. Our gospel songs were being played just one day a week, on Sundays. Mainstream radio ignored gospel the other 6 days of the week. It's hard to make a living when your records are being played only one day a week, and I wanted our music to be heard every day.

Tommy Fairchild decided to leave the group in '72, so I started looking for a new piano player who I thought could round out our new sound. I called a man named Tony Brown, who I had met for the first time, 10 years earlier. At that time, Tony was 16 years old and was playing at an all-night gospel sing. He was so small that he sat on a big phone book as he played the piano. He may have been small in stature, but I could see that he was a huge talent, even way back then.

By '72, Tony was playing with the Blackwood Brothers. Before James Blackwood offered him a job, he had been with J.D. Sumner and the Stamps Quartet. I called Tony and offered him a job with the Oaks, and he said yes. As I was writing this book, I thought it would be good to talk to Tony, to see what he remembered of our time together. Here are some of his memories:

"When I was a kid, the only thing I listened to was southern gospel music. And when I think of the icons of southern gospel, I think of Jake Hess, Hovie Lister, J.D.

Sumner and William Lee Golden. William has a charisma, not only from the way he looks, but in the way he talks to you. He's always had that.

When William Lee offered me a job with the Oak Ridge Boys, I jumped at it. J.D. Sumner had been my all-time hero, and working with J.D. and the Stamps Quartet was my dream job. But the Oak Ridge Boys were cooler. They had a killer band, and they wore in-style clothes and had long hair. They looked like rock stars. The Oak Ridge Boys were cutting edge and they pushed the envelope.

Gary McSpadden had looked like Elvis, and the first time I met William, he looked like Warren Beatty. I thought, "All of the Oaks' baritone singers are so cool." When I first joined the Oak Ridge Boys, William was Mr. G.Q.

I was with the Oaks for almost 2 years, until I got a job playing piano for Elvis. But I kept a real relationship and friendship with William Lee. He's the only person since my gospel music years who I've stayed in touch with, on a very personal basis. We've continued to talk on the phone 4 or 5 times a month, every month, or we would visit in person at each other's homes.

You meet a few people in your life who make an impression on you and they really affect you. William really affected the way I look at myself, the way I presented myself, and what I wore. He made me want to be somebody.

Anytime I had life problems, I had just a few people I would call for counsel, and William was one of them. He has been through so much, and always gave such honest and well thought-out advice. He was the go-to person for me. If I was having some kind of trouble, he was the man I would go to.

> William Lee is a star. When he walks in the room, head's turn. He has reinvented himself numerous times, and he became cooler with each reinvention. But he's also just a great person. He's peaceful and quiet, and he's got a Gandhi thing going. He's like a cool version of Gandhi."
>
> — Tony Brown

After Tony left the Oaks, he played piano for Elvis until Elvis' death. Then Tony went on to become one of the greatest record producers in country music, or any other form of music.

Tony Brown was much closer to Elvis Presley than I was, but I did get to meet Elvis a few times. I met him backstage in Vegas two times, and before that, he came to the gospel quartet conventions we were singing at. Elvis loved gospel music. J.D. Sumner, hosted the quartet convention in Elvis' hometown of Memphis. The Blackwood Brothers and the Statesmen also helped host the event, and Elvis loved all those groups. He wanted to watch the concerts, but he didn't want to create a scene, so they built a little booth just for him at the side of the stage. He could watch the show through a little window and people in the audience couldn't see him. Elvis also attended the quartet convention in Nashville.

By 1972, Noel Fox was wanting to get off the road. I tried to talk him out of it. I told him that he had been with us through our tough years, but I had no doubt that all of our hard work was about to pay off. I told him my vision of where the group was heading, and the hit records we would soon be having. But Noel gave his notice, and I told him I'd start looking for a new bass singer. I knew my search wasn't going to take long, because I had only one man in mind.

Richard Sterban and I had met when he was with the Keystone Quartet out of Buffalo, New York, and I thought he had the perfect voice for the Oak Ridge Boys. I respected Richard's talent and he was one of my favorite bass singers. He had a quality in his voice that was quite unique. He has a rich quality to his voice that a lot of bass singers don't have.

I became friends with Richard when I put the Keystones on some shows I was promoting, and I also brought them to the International Gospel Music Festival. Richard had always been a fan of the Oak Ridge Boys and his Keystone Quartet sang a lot of our songs in their concerts. Richard's career had come a long way since the Keystones, and he was now with J.D. Sumner and the Stamps quartet, who were a big part of the Elvis Presley show. J.D.'s low bass notes were legendary, and when Richard joined The Stamps, Elvis had the two most impressive bass voices in any form of music.

Singing behind Elvis was a pretty amazing job, but I thought I had an even better one for Richard. Richard gives his version of the decision that changed his life:

"In 1972, I was singing with Elvis and J.D. Sumner and the Stamps, and I was on top of the world. The time I spent with Elvis was such a special time. I will never forget the time I spent singing for the King of Rock and Roll. But out of the blue, I got a phone call from William Lee Golden. William told me he was looking for a front-line bass singer, who was going to be a star of their show.

I was a big fan of the Oak Ridge Boys, and William spoke about some of the possibilities for the future of the group. He shared the vision he had for the group and where he wanted them to go in the future. I could tell that he thought the success they were going to reach was just unlimited, and I wanted to be a part of it.

William's optimistic and positive outlook was a factor in my decision to join the group.

At the end of our conversation, I told William, 'Give me some time to think it over. This is a major decision in my life.' But I knew right then that I was going to take the job. I wanted to be a part of the Oak Ridge Boys, but I waited until the next day to call him back to accept the offer.

So, I made the decision to leave Elvis and join the Oaks Ridge Boys. I can't believe that almost 50 years have passed since then. It has been an amazing five decades, and I owe a whole lot to William Lee Golden for making that phone call to ask me to join the group. It was a call that really changed my life."

— Richard Sterban

We offered Richard the exact same "king's ransom" he was making singing with Elvis...$275 a week! But Richard's decision to join us paid off almost instantly. He ended up being the headlining act in the same big arenas and coliseums that Elvis had played. If he had stayed with Elvis, at best, Richard would have been backup to J.D. Sumner. And if he had still been there when Elvis died, who knows what would have happened to Richard. The world may have never heard of him, and that would have been a loss.

The same year Richard joined us, we played the Utah State Fair. I still have a poster from that event. All the entertainment was free with the fair admission of $1.50. For a dollar and a half, you could see Lynn Anderson, Tammy Wynette and George Jones, Ray Price, and Bobby Vinton at the fair. They were all the headliners who came in for one night each. The Oak Ridge Boys were not headliners in the grandstand. Instead, we performed at a smaller bandstand in the middle of the fair, and we performed 3 to 4 shows every day, for 10 straight days!

We might have been on the smaller stage, but we were making a big impact. We were at the peak of our gospel music career and were trying to reach the next rung. Just a few years later, we would return to the Utah State Fair to play the big grandstand. As we walked out on stage, I said to myself, "We have gone from the bandstand to the grandstand."

The Oak Ridge Boys were a wholesome and clean family show. You knew it was safe to bring your kids to our concerts. And our live shows got a lot more entertaining when we hired a new guy in 1973. His name was Joe Bonsall. He was a streetwise kid from Philly.

Little Willie Wynn had an offer to be part of an airplane business, so he chose to leave the group. We knew that replacing fan favorite Little Willie would not be easy. He was one of the most popular tenor singers in gospel music. But I thought that Joe Bonsall was just the guy who could fill Little Willie's big shoes. I had met Joe when he and Richard Sterban were both in the Keystone Quartet. Joe had also booked the Oaks for some concerts in Pennsylvania, and I had gotten the Keystones to open for us on quite a few shows. Joe and I had talked on the phone many times and I always enjoyed our visits.

Duane also knew Joe well, as he had produced Joe's group in his recording studio. Duane produced 10 different albums on the Keystones. He was so impressed with them that he signed the Keystones to his record label, Superior Records. He really built his label around the Keystone Quartet. Back then, Duane produced and recorded a lot of smaller groups or part-time acts. Then he pressed their albums himself. He was a one-man record company.

When we replaced Willie with Joe, it was an unusual switch. They were two totally different type of singers. Little Willie was a tenor singer from birth and Joe is more of a lead singer who has a high voice. Joe could sing tenor, but he didn't have the screechy, high tenor voice that some guys have. He could really belt out a tune, and his voice appeals to a broad audience. Joe also has a raw, intimate way of delivering a song.

Since Joe was the leader of the Keystone Quartet, when he joined us, that kind of ended their group. We also got pianist Garland Craft from the Keystones. Garland would stay with us from our gospel days well into many of our big country hits. Of course, we had already gotten Richard, so a lot of people looked at the Keystones as kind of a farm club for the Oak Ridge Boys.

I called Joe and asked him to come to Nashville to try out for the Oak Ridge Boys. He was one I really wanted in the group. I'll let him pick it up from there:

"Many times in life, we have important decisions to make. They are life-changing choices like taking a new job or moving to a different state. Sometimes we don't know which way we should go. But when William Lee called to offer me a job with the Oak Ridge Boys, I didn't have to think twice. It was the call I was praying would come.

Not only was I a fan of the group, but I was also good friends with William, Duane and Richard. I had promoted some Oak Ridge Boys shows up in the Niagara Frontier, and I got to know them all. Richard had been a member of my Keystone Quartet, so we were already very close. Duane had started producing the Keystones on his record label. He basically started the label because of the Keystones, and we were close.

I became friends with William Lee when he booked my group, The Keystone Quartet to perform at the International Song Festival he was hosting in Nashville. I was excited to be performing at such a big event, but when the festival was over, I returned to my little apartment in Buffalo, New York. I wanted our group to have the success the Oak Ridge Boys were having, but we were barely making enough to pay our bills.

> I've never talked about this, but it was then that the Keystones had a bus wreck that changed our lives. No one was killed, but a few people were seriously hurt. After that accident, my heart just wasn't with the Keystones anymore. During that time, William Lee would call me late at night. He could tell I was discouraged, so he spoke about the importance of following your dreams. Golden was very inspiring to me.
>
> So, when William Lee offered me the job, it was a true 'no-brainer.' I couldn't get packed fast enough. I was headed to Nashville, to sing with my heroes."
>
> — Joe Bonsall

Joe had a lot of great qualities. He still does. He has a rawness to his singing, and he sings from his heart. He was influenced by pop, rock and roll, and gospel music.

There is a wide variety of styles for gospel tenors. Some have an Irish folk sound, and some have a big, bold opera sound. But Joe was different. He had grown up listening to that early rock and pop sound that was played on Dick Clark's American Bandstand in Philadelphia. To me, he has a rock and roll voice, instead of an operatic tenor voice.

With me, Richard, Duane, and Joe, along with our great band, we now had the sound that would eventually evolve into what we became in country music.

FROM GOSPEL TO THE GODFATHER

With the arrival of Joe Bonsall, the final piece of our group member puzzle was in place. The Oak Ridge Boys were now ready to set the gospel music world on its ear. And we did.

The Oaks won every award gospel music offered, including the 1974 Grammy Award for Best Gospel Performance for "The Baptism of Jesse Taylor." Our records were going to the top of the charts and our live shows were selling out everywhere we went. After each concert, our audiences were going home, telling their friends and family about the exciting concert they had just attended.

A lot of the gospel acts used only a piano player or sang with "tracks" of pre-recorded music. Of course, that was much cheaper, but when we put our big group of live musicians on stage with us, we just electrified our audiences.

I saw our group as entertainers. I had no interest in preaching to people. I wanted to entertain them. I was not attracted to gospel music because of the preaching. That was not my calling. My calling was entertaining. I was attracted to the music and the singing. I was also attracted to the fun the gospel singers were having. When I went to the all-night gospel sings when I was a teenager, I was going to have fun, and those singers were entertainers back in the day.

During that time, we caught the attention of one of Country Music's greatest entertainers…Johnny Cash. In 1971, Johnny invited us to be on his network TV show. Then he asked us to open some shows for him, and also sing backup for him during those shows. Johnny was a mega superstar at the time and playing in front of his huge crowds was like nothing we had ever seen. Johnny's kindness gave us the chance to introduce ourselves and our music to tens of thousands of people.

In '73, Johnny asked us to sing on a single with him and the Carter Family. It was called "Praise the Lord, and Pass the Soup." That song marked the first time the Oak Ridge Boys made it on the Country Music charts. I will talk more about Johnny in a little while, but for now, I will say that Johnny Cash was a one-of-a-kind. I treasure my memories of our friendship. Johnny took us everywhere he played, including the hotel casinos of Las Vegas. Imagine…a gospel music group singing in a casino in Sin City! How cool is that?

But making a living in gospel music is not easy, even if you are the hottest act in the genre. With all our awards and gospel hit songs, we were still barely making enough money to pay our bills. And while our big group of musicians was impressive, that also meant the small amount of money we made had to be divided up among 6, 7 or 8 people.

We also started noticing something else. While our fans loved our longer hair and more current, stylish stage clothes, many of the other gospel acts began to (not so quietly) voice their disdain for us. As I heard their comments that "The Oak Ridge Boys don't belong in gospel music," I totally agreed.

I felt that we had reached our peak in gospel. We were a big fish in a small pond, and I wanted to be a big fish in a great big pond…one the size of an ocean. In December of 1974, I did an interview with the Nashville Tennessean newspaper. I told them I thought we had gone as far as we could go in gospel music, and I wanted to record a secular record.

My words caused quite an uproar, but I was just being honest. Almost every gospel act I knew also enjoyed country music, but they were afraid to sing it in public. I thought it was ironic that back then, many of the big country music acts included at least one gospel song on every album they did. They weren't afraid to sing gospel, but gospel performers were petrified to sing a country song.

Our band member Greg Gordon wrote a wonderful, straight country song called "Bringing It Back." There was nothing gospel about it at all. But I talked the other guys into recording it. It turned out great, but we couldn't get it played on the radio. A year later, Elvis Presley recorded the song, and it has been "an Elvis song" ever since. But the Oak Ridge Boys did it first.

I never looked at it as the Oak Ridge Boys were trying to leave gospel. But we were so limited there, and we were just trying to expand our music. We wanted to take gospel music to a higher place, to reach people that it hadn't been reaching. I still loved to sing gospel songs and we had always planned to continue including those in our concerts. But I thought more people would come out to hear us sing those gospel songs, if we also sang other types of music.

But most radio programmers and concert promoters didn't agree. As we started recording more secular and less preachy type songs, we found that gospel DJs and concert bookers didn't like it, because we were "too country," and we "worked with Johnny Cash." And country radio DJs and bookers didn't want us because we were "that gospel act." With us now caught in the middle, our record sales and concert bookings started to plummet.

Our manager, Don Light dropped us. He had been trying to book gospel dates for us, but he said concert promoters couldn't grasp what we were trying to do. They resented the more progressive style of music we were doing. I knew that we needed someone who could get my vision of what we wanted to do.

I explained to anyone who would listen, "We have been trying to walk back and forth between gospel and country music. But there comes a time when we need to walk completely through the door into country music, slam the door shut behind us and stay there."

I was on my own with that idea for a couple years as we tried to survive the no man's land between gospel and country music. One person who did agree with me was my wife. I'd share my dreams for our group with her and she would encourage and push me, saying, "I have no doubt you can do it." Then she added, "But you need to have everyone on the same page. This is a team effort. Joe, Richard and Duane all chose to do this with their lives, just like you did. You have to be a team."

Joe and Richard were the next to come on board with my vision. They were ready to "go country." But Duane held back. He wanted to stay in gospel music. Duane was of one the most popular men in gospel music at the time. He had won the "Mr. Gospel Music" fan awards, and he thought we should keep doing what had brought us success in the past.

In one last effort to do that, in 1974, I met a guy who promoted the International Song Festival in Saratoga Springs, New York. His name was Larry Goldblatt and he fell in love with the Oak Ridge Boys. Larry had managed a bunch of big-name pop and rock acts, including Blood, Sweat and Tears. Larry wanted to manage us, so we hired him, and he came to Nashville and spent a few months with us.

Larry loved promoting and knew everyone in the "big leagues" of show business. But the gospel music world was totally foreign to him, and he didn't really know what to do with us. He handled us for 6 months, before we parted ways.

We continued to struggle, and when things got really tough, Duane and I started trying to liquidate anything we could sell in order to get enough money to keep us going. We went to Johnny Cash and asked him to buy our publishing company, and he turned us down. Then he gave us some priceless advice, saying, "I believe in you guys. If you don't believe in yourselves, no one else will either. You've got to stick it out until everyone finally realizes how great you are."

I listened to Johnny, and during our hard times, even during our very leanest and hardest times, I never, ever thought about quitting. I never considered giving up on the group. I didn't want to go back home a failure. I would have rather been a failure on the road than to go back home as a failure.

Johnny assured us he would do all he could to help us, by continuing to have us on as many of his shows as possible. During that time, Duane was also still trying to book us some gospel dates. But God works in mysterious ways, and God was about to use an unlikely source as a way to get the Oak Ridge Boys all on the same page.

We were heading to Las Vegas to open for "The Man in Black," but the night before that, we played the big coliseum in Roanoke, Virginia. We were one of a bunch of gospel acts on the bill that night. As we waited to go on, we watched The Kingsmen Quartet performing. We stood at the side of the stage, as the leader of The Kingsmen, Jim Hammill, (ironically, the former Oak Ridge Boy whose place I took) announced to the crowd, "Turn the lights up. This ain't no night club. We've got a group here that sings in casinos and night clubs." We all just looked at each other as he started going on about our long hair and us being rock and roll singers. We couldn't believe it.

After trying to block out what had just happened, we walked out to sing. And 300 people got up and walked out. We did our show, and as soon as we finished, Duane said, "Get this bus to Vegas. I don't care if we ever do another gospel show again."

Yes, God works in mysterious ways.

It's ironic that our country group has now probably sung gospel music to more people than just about any gospel act ever did. Country music fans love gospel music too. I know I do. And the Oak Ridge Boys will always love singing at least one or two gospel songs in every show we do.

People sometimes ask, "If you hadn't been a singer, what would you have been?" Well, I had no "Plan B" or backup plan. But if I had to come up with an answer, I guess I might have been a hairdresser or barber. That might sound laughable coming from the guy who hasn't cut his hair or beard in 40 years. But I actually cut all the Oaks' hair until 1977. I also styled the band's hair and cut my son's hair.

When I was young, I cut my grandpa's hair several times. It was a mess the first time I did it, and I was learning as I went. When I got going with those clippers, I could get off track pretty fast. But I slowly learned how to operate the scissors and clippers and learned how to use the comb to lift the hair as I cut it. The Oaks would do long tours and were away from home for a month or more. Back then, everyone was clean cut and we had to keep up with our haircuts. I also cut Laverne Tripp's and some other gospel folk's hair. A few people were scared to sit down in front of me for the first time, but I loved to cut hair.

Once we had all committed to giving everything we had toward a country music career, we knew there was one last piece of our puzzle that was missing. We would find that missing piece in 1975, when we met Jim Halsey. At the time, Jim Halsey ran the biggest country music booking agency in the world. His main office was in Tulsa, Oklahoma, but he also had an office in Hollywood, and then he added an office in Nashville.

Jim can tell that part of the story better than I can:

"I was managing Roy Clark, Mel Tillis and Freddy Fender when I met the Oak Ridge Boys in Nashville. Columbia Records was having a showcase, introducing new artists, and the Oaks were one of the last acts to perform and by the time they went on, a lot of the crowd had left. When I first saw them, I thought, 'Wow, these guys sure have a modern, hip look for a gospel group.' I was impressed with their look, but when they started to perform, I was just blown away.

When they finished, I went backstage, and introduced myself to them. I said, 'If you're ever interested in expanding your repertoire and singing more than just gospel, maybe some pop or country, I would be interested in working with you.'

A couple weeks later, I got a call from William Lee. William was, and still is a guy who can see the future and he sees a future with no limitations. He told me that he knew the group was capable of selling a huge amount of records, as long as they had a manager who believed in them, and who could get them a major record company who would get behind them. I assured him I was that person.

My company put on what we called 'The Halsey Company Ranch Party.' We invited all the important people in the business, from the show buyers to press people and industry VIPs to come spend the weekend at our ranch. It was a big showcase for all the artists we represented. Hank Thompson, Roy Clark and Tammy Wynette were all part of our Ranch Party, and we also had the Oak Ridge Boys on the show.

Most of the people in the audience had never heard of the Oak Ridge Boys, or if they did, they thought they were just a gospel act. I was doing a lot of business with Jim Foglesong at Dot Records. Jim was president of the

> label. I already told him about the Oaks, but when he saw them do their thing on our showcase, he was just bowled over. He turned to me and said, 'I get it Jim. Let's do it. I want to sign them to our record company.'
>
> — Jim Halsey

The Oak Ridge Boys were another step closer to their destiny, thanks to two Jims. Jim Foglesong was the man who believed in us enough to sign us to a major record label. And Jim Halsey was the man who believed in us more than anyone on the planet.

Jim Halsey was, and is the key element to the success of the Oak Ridge Boys. He is one of the most important elements of our longevity. When we joined forces with Halsey, there was nothing that could stop us. We made a handshake agreement with him and our relationship is based on that handshake and on our word. Jim is so important to our past, our present and our future.

Thank God I found Jim Halsey. He is the one guy who had faith in me and whose dreams were just as big as mine. When I shared my vision with Jim, he not only saw it too, but he could even see how he could enhance my dreams and visions, and make them even bigger. He said I wasn't dreaming big enough! No one had ever told me that before. Jim was the ultimate visionary.

A year after joining up with Jim as a country act, we won a Grammy Award...ironically for Best Gospel Performance on the song "Where the Soul Never Dies." It was actually a contemporary-gospel rock song, and we asked Charlie Daniels to play on it with us. He already had the Charlie Daniels Band going, but he was still playing some recording sessions for other people. He hadn't had any of his own big hits yet. Charlie played a slide solo that really stood out on our song.

We were thankful to be honored by the Grammy voters. But we were still searching for our first big success with a country song. Jim Halsey had a saying that he preached to us, "The Oak Ridge Boys are just 3 minutes away from being the biggest stars in America." So, we continued looking for that 3-minute song that would put us on our way.

In January of 1976, Jim put us on our way for a 3-week trip that would change our lives. As the USA prepared to celebrate its 200th year of freedom, we were headed to the one place where no one was free. Roy Clark and the Oak Ridge Boys did a 21-day tour of the Soviet Union.

Before we left, we met with officials from the U.S. State Department who told us what we should expect. But even with those warnings, we had no idea what we were about to see. At the time, there was no relationship of any kind between Russia and the U.S., and if there were any conversations between the two Super Powers, they were always hostile. The only thing colder than Russia-U.S. relations was the temperature. When we landed in Moscow, it was a balmy 20 degrees below zero.

From Moscow, we took a rickety, 1920s train to Riga Latvia, where we spent a week. Then we went to Leningrad for 7 days and then back to Moscow for our last week. As we arrived behind "The Iron Curtain," it was like stepping back in time 50 or 60 years. It was unbelievable, and it was a very sobering experience for us. One of the first things I saw was an old woman on top of a two-story house. She was shoveling snow off the roof. I couldn't imagine my mother having to do something like that.

For the next few weeks, we received a first-hand lesson on the true scourge of socialism and communism. The Russian people were basically slaves to the government. No one in Russia was allowed to own anything. The government owned everything…including the people. The Soviet population couldn't buy their own homes or cars. The government "allowed" residents to have a refrigerator and stove, but they didn't really belong to the people. If the authorities decided they needed a refrigerator somewhere else, they would just come in and take it. If your icebox stopped working, you had to do government paperwork to apply for a new refrigerator, and it might be a couple years before they allowed you to get another one.

There was no public worship allowed, and don't even ask about healthcare in the Soviet Union. We watched how the strict communist government kept the people down. The government intruded in everything. Then they intruded on us. Even though our tour was billed as a cultural exchange program, we were all instructed to never leave our hotel room when we were not performing. I thought it was odd that none of our hotel rooms had locks on the doors…but I would soon find out the reason.

Joe and I were sharing a room. He had a small, single bed and I had another. Joe was reading the book "Helter Skelter," when our door burst open. I yelled, "What the hell?!" Three heavily armed members of the KGB spent the next 15 minutes searching our room. One had some sort of metal detector that he took all over our suitcases and clothing,

We would also have another interesting run in with the KGB. Before we performed, we had to turn in the lyrics to all the songs we were going to sing. The authorities read through all of them and had to give their approval to each one before we could sing it on stage.

When they got to our Grammy award winning "Where the Soul Never Dies," they demanded that we change the words "To Canaan Land I'm on my way, where the soul of man never dies." They told us to replace "Canaan Land" with "Disneyland!" We refused. But we did a quick rewrite and instead of singing, "To Canaan Land," we sang, "To that fair land."

Our Russia tour turned out to be a highlight of our career and of our lives. It was truly incredible. Huge crowds turned out to see us. They filled big auditoriums, even though no one could understand a word of what we were singing. But they could feel the music, especially when we let our bass singer loose. They could feel Richard Sterban's low notes! Every night, we watched from the stage as our music was able to reach beyond the language barrier we had.

We won those crowds over, and we turned the audiences, not only into country music fans, but we also made them fans of America. We were told by many leaders in Washington that Roy Clark and the Oak Ridge Boys were able to break through diplomatically between the U.S. and the Soviet Union, in a way that no political figure ever could.

I loved every minute of our Russia tour, but I couldn't wait to get back to the land of the free. When we returned to America, we came back much more patriotic and much more thankful for the freedoms we have here in the United States. I had been raised to love our country, but my short time in Russia made me love it so much more.

More than 45 years have passed since that trip. A lot has changed in Russia and the U.S. since then. I have to admit that the evolution of things in our country today is quite concerning. I know that a lot of young people are buying into the big lie that socialism is good. It is not. To see the political evolution and platforms that are being promoted today, makes me sad and angry. I have no doubt some of those moves will strip us of our freedom and opportunities. I wish those who support such ideas could have been with us when we visited the Soviet Union.

Jim Halsey's idea of a country music goodwill tour to the Soviet Union had become a reality. Yes, Jim is a visionary. He is also a gentle soul and spirit. He is always positive, and I've never seen him angry. The most memorable example of that…the time if there was ever one for him to become negative or angry, came on July 7, 1979, on a show he booked us in Switzerland.

We were part of a month-long music festival, and our date featured Doc Watson, Barbara Mandrell, The Oak Ridge Boys and Roy Clark. It was a day we will always remember, and I'm sure it is one that Barbara Mandrell will never forget.

As we arrived at the venue, someone mentioned that "these are fans of TRADITIONAL country music." That should have been a warning. Doc Watson was the first performer that day. He played his guitar and the crowd loved him. The crowd really went wild for his music. But then things changed...for the worse.

Barbara Mandrell came out and went into her razzamatazz country show, and that crowd started booing and hissing. She did another song and they booed even more. And they kept booing until she ran off the stage in tears. Irby Mandrell, Barbara's dad told the press, "The crowd was a bunch of barbarians."

Richard, Joe, Duane and I all looked at each other, knowing we were the next victims to be sent out to the lions. But out we went. And we never stopped. We went from one song into another, without pausing. After the first song, some people were cheering and clapping, but we could hear boos that were just as loud. From there on, we never stopped for a second in between songs. We didn't wait for any applause because we knew the boos would drown out any clapping.

We managed to survive to the end of our set, and just before Roy Clark went out to close the show, Duane whispered to him, "You won't be able to sing your slow songs." Roy responded, "I damn sure will."

When he walked out on stage, Roy told the crowd, "Hey, you were rude to some of my friends. We've come 10, 000 miles to play for you, and that's not really the reception we were expecting. But I'm going to do a few songs for you." He really scolded them like a teacher would. Then he started his show with the slowest song he had. They never booed him one time.

We never went back to Switzerland. I'm pretty sure Barbara Mandrell never returned either. But I have the feeling they're not missing us much.

But even this incident was not enough to change Jim Halsey's always positive, never angry demeanor. What was his reaction when we got back to the U.S.? He announced, "I produced that show and I think this is one of the most successful things we have ever done. The crowd was expecting more of the old-time country stuff, and they didn't know any of us. But there was so much press and media coverage there and this is going to open the door to international records and TV shows." He continued, "I don't look at that as any type of failure for the Oak Ridge Boys or Barbara Mandrell. The audience might not have gotten us that night, but we were able to get our message across around the world."

Some of the first shows Jim Halsey booked for us were in casinos. We played the showroom of the Landmark Hotel in Las Vegas for 3 to 4 weeks at a time, as we headlined a show called "Country Music USA." The Landmark Hotel was just across the street from the Las Vegas Hilton, where Elvis was playing. Richard Sterban made a call and asked if he could bring us over to meet Elvis. Thanks to Richard, we were all able to experience Elvis' charisma and magnetism in person.

When we weren't in Vegas, Jim had us touring across the country with some of country music's biggest names. We opened shows for Roy Clark and Freddy Fender. We did shows with Marty Robbins, Minnie Pearl and a tour of the Pacific Northwest with Buck Owens and the Buckaroos.

Jim Halsey had already found out about the power of television. He used TV to turn Roy Clark into a superstar, and now he would do the same with the Oak Ridge Boys. Jim hired Dick Howard and Judy Pofsky, and added a TV department in Los Angeles, and they concentrated just on booking TV shows. Thanks especially to Dick's efforts, they were able to get us on all the big network TV shows.

Even while we were still singing what I would call "secular gospel", and before we had any country hits, Jim was able to get us on The Merv Griffin and Dinah Shore shows. We appeared on the popular Mike Douglas Show almost 30 times, and we even guest hosted the show with Mike. After conquering all the daytime TV shows, we became regulars on The Tonight Show with Johnny Carson. We did that show time after time, and during each of those shows, we almost always got to sing two songs. No matter how many times we were on with Johnny Carson, it was intimidating when I thought about how many people were going to see his very popular show.

To me, television was the magic of getting the Oak Ridge Boys in front of millions of people. We wanted to show what we did in concert, when we got in front of any television cameras. I felt if people could see what we did, they would want to buy a ticket to our show or they would want to buy our record.

In the late '70s and through the '80s, if you turned on any big music TV show, you would have seen the Oak Ridge Boys. Remember The Midnight Special? We did it. Dick Clark's Rockin' New Year's Eve? We were there. Don Kirschner's Rock Concert? A country group on the Rock Concert? Yep, we rocked 'em. How about the disco-ish Solid Gold show? We sang as the Solid Gold Dancers boogied! We did about 10 episodes of Solid Gold! And don't forget The Dukes of Hazard…which we did two times. And today, we're fortunate to

76

still do a lot of TV. We probably do as many national TV shows as any of the younger, chart-topping acts.

Over the last four decades, Jim Halsey became so important to the Oak Ridge Boys, that we started calling him The Godfather. As I was writing this book, Jim celebrated his 90th birthday. And just like the Oak Ridge Boys, he has not slowed down. He is still as sharp as a tack and still works full-time. How many other 90 year-olds can say that? He is still just as hands on as he ever was in our career. Each day, Jim is still coming up with wonderful ideas, and he shares those with the booking agents, the record label and public relations people. He's sending emails constantly throughout the day, even on weekends keeping us all up to date on the latest concert or TV show he has booked for us.

Sometimes in life, things happen that are a godsend. That's what it was when we met Jim Halsey.

MY THREE SONS…
With One More To Come Later

When I'm gone, all of my material possessions will be scattered or thrown away. The only thing that will remain will be my children and grandchildren. Our children are the fruits of the love of their parents. I always felt love, support and nurturing from my parents, and I wanted my sons to feel the same thing.

The old saying, "The apple didn't fall far from the tree" truly applies to me and my sons. There's no doubt of where they came from. I love all my kids. My greatest treasures are my children and grandchildren.

Rusty, Chris and Craig were all born when I was farming and working at the paper mill in Brewton. I was also singing on the weekends, so I was gone most of the time. But it was always a joy to come home to those three boys.

Rusty loved music early on. When he was a little boy, he would turn old potato chip cans into a set of tom-toms. He was into drumming and I got him a good set of drums. As a little kid, he was into all music. He was touched by the words and melodies of the songs.

Rusty had an up-close view when the Oak Ridge Boys made the move from gospel to country music. Here are some of his thoughts on those days:

"I played drums for the Oaks when I was just 8 years old. It was my first time on stage, and I knew at that moment, that this was what I wanted to do for a living. I wanted to be a musician.

I didn't listen to Oak Ridge Boys records at home, but they were electrifying to watch in concert. There would be an auditorium of gospel music fans, filled with 1, 000 people and when you're 8 years old, 1, 000 people is like a hundred thousand. So, they were always big stars to me.

When I was a senior in high school, I became a full member of the band. It was 1976, and they were going on their Russia tour. While they were in the Soviet Union, I went to night school and got my diploma, so that when they came back, I could join them on their first headlining gig at the Landmark Hotel in Las Vegas. I started out as a utility man, playing whatever they needed, including rhythm guitar, congas, tambourine, percussion, and accessary keyboards.

There was nothing more fun for me, and I think I speak for a few others, when I say, it was such a magical time, when it was everyone on one bus. When they got so big, that they needed two buses, and they split up with the 4 guys on one bus and the band on the other, we kind of split up in other ways. But it was magical during those lean days on one bus.

When the Oaks had the "Y'all Comeback Saloon," I was out playing piano with Larry Gatlin. His career was just taking off and I played on his "Love Is Just a Game" album. I was credited on the album with my real full name of William Lee Golden, Jr.

I had started out thinking I was going to be a drummer, but after seeing Elton John in concert at the Nashville Municipal Auditorium, I put my sticks down and started playing piano. I never had a lesson, but with Elton as my inspiration, I taught myself to play. From there, I started writing songs when I was 19. The Oak Ridge Boys recorded 3 of those. Two were on their Platinum "Bobbie Sue" album and the other was the title cut for their "Christmas Again" album.

My dad loves what he does. The fans love him, and he loves them just as much. I've seen him sign autographs for the last person. He's known for that. He always told me that the people he's signing for are the ones who are going to buy tickets to the show the next time the group comes to town. That attitude throughout his career, has made him a beloved entertainer."

— Rusty Golden

All my kids spent the summers on our family farm in Alabama. My older sons were able to spend time with my mother and father there. They followed their grandpa around all day, and they saw what a hard worker he was, as he was on the go from 5 a.m. to 10 p.m.

When I was growing up, our family didn't take any vacations. My dad was always working on the farm and didn't have time to take any trip. The biggest vacation I had as a boy was a 90-mile Greyhound bus trip from Brewton to Mobile. When I became a father, my family didn't take many vacations either. I was singing on the road all the time, so when I got home, the last thing I wanted to do was travel somewhere. I'm sure my wife and kids would have liked to take a little trip somewhere, but it didn't happen.

I asked my son Chris to share a few of his memories of those years:

"We didn't take many family vacations. We went to the Memphis Zoo for one day. We fed the monkeys and came home! We didn't stay the night. That was our vacation, and one time, we went to Rock City for a day trip. But I did get to go out on the road with dad when the Oak Ridge Boys had a close date like Paducah and Bowling Green, Kentucky or Memphis.

I was in the 5th grade at Good Pasture School, and the Oaks' tour bus pulled in to pick me up. Dad and Duane got off the bus and came walking down the hall. They were dressed in their stage suits and all the teachers, especially the female teachers just went gaga over them.

I rode the bus with them to Memphis. While dad and the rest of the group was setting up and getting ready for the concert, I went walking on Beale Street, by myself. In a store window, I saw a pair of patent leather and suede shoes. They were stacked high heels and cost $40.00. I ran back and asked dad if I could buy them. He gave me the money and I walked back down to Beale Street, again, all by myself and bought them. My mom never let him live that down as she asked, 'You let a 10 year-old walk by himself in downtown Memphis?'

I always thought the Oak Ridge Boys were as big as the Beatles. There was a lot of people who came to see their gospel shows back then, and those big crowds looked even larger to a little boy.

The group once did a show for an assembly at our school. That show affected so many of my friends, and for at least one, it was life changing. After the concert, my classmate, Adam Hampton sent a letter to dad. He drew a picture of the band and wrote, "One of these days, I want to play in a band and ride on a bus like that." Adam went on to play for Ronnie Milsap for 20 years, and he is now in Sara Evans' band.

When we moved to our home on Indian Lake Road in Hendersonville, all 3 of us boys shared the same bedroom. We had 3 little, twin beds lined up, like Goldilocks and the 3 little bears. We slept like that until Rusty was 14 years old, and then he got to move into another room.

But that room was usually occupied with a rotating guest. Duane Allen's wife Norah Lee stayed with us before they were married. Greg Gordon lived with us for a couple years when he was singing with the Imperials. The Samuelsons from Sweden stayed with us when they visited the US. Joe Bonsall also stayed with us when he first joined the group. We had a revolving door at our house.

While mom did most of the work in raising us, dad also did his share. He cut my hair until I was 15. He was a good barber. There is one funny memory that came up as I was thinking about dad writing this book: He never wore blue jeans when I was growing up. One day, mom bought him a pair of blue jeans, and he looked at them and asked, 'What are these dungarees for?' She answered, 'I thought you could wear them around the house.' He said, 'I had to wear them every day of my life until I was 18 years old. And I don't plan to wear a pair of these ever again. You take them back and get your money back.' But over the last 20 years, he changed his tune and jeans are about the only thing he wears today.

Dad was always a great supporter of everything we did. He was sweet and loved to have fun, and he was always the coolest dad in the room. He still is."

— Chris Golden

A few years ago, my son Craig stopped shaving and cutting his hair. Almost overnight, he looked exactly like me. And like me, Craig is quiet and is usually a man of few words. But he agreed to say a few here:

"People come up and ask, 'Anybody ever tell you that you look like that guy from the Oak Ridge Boys?' I laugh and say, 'No, I've never heard that.' Then I say, 'Yeah, that's my dad.'

As I was growing up, dad taught me right from wrong. He taught me to be honest. He always stressed, 'Don't lie. If someone lies to you, they will cheat you and steal from you too.' He taught me about God. Mom took me to church all the time, and between the two of them, I had the guidance I needed to get through life.

I'm so glad I had the parents that I did. They were the best. My dad was the best dad in the world and my mom was the best mom in the world. I used to hear kids at school say they hated their parents, and I couldn't understand that. I loved my parents so much.

I want to be more like my dad. My grandfather, dad's father was the finest guy I ever knew. He was one of the best men who ever walked on the planet. And my dad is a lot like his dad. He is such a good person. He is honest, loving and super smart. I love my dad."

— Craig Golden

Four-year-old William Lee Golden, standing on my grandpa's car.

William Lee Golden, 193

One of my earliest photos. I spent most of my childhood barefooted.

ly grandparents
lizabeth and
ee Rush
olden, holding
eir triplets
Matthew, Mark
nd Luke, my
ther.

My mother and
father, Ruth and
Luke Golden.

With my sister
Lanette, 1943.

Not real thrilled with
one of my first photo
shoots.

An early school photo.

School Days
1944 ~ 45

At my grandparent's house. May 1949

My last GI haircut.

Recovering from a bike accident.

This Olan Mills portrait was one of my mother's favorites.

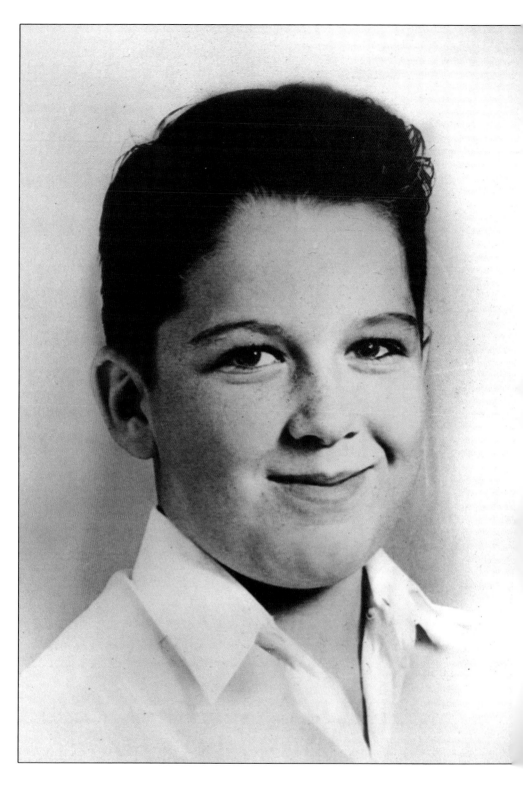

My first color photo at 11 years old.

School Days

1952-53

Some of the school photos were more like mug shots.

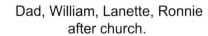
Dad, William, Lanette, Ronnie after church.

All smiles with my father and little brother Ronnie.

Doing my chores o
the farm, July 1953

Lanette and I show off our new mandolin and guitar.

Posing with my sister
Lanette.

Proud of my first suit.

Our family didn't have much money, but my father wanted us to have nice clothes.

"William, whatever you do, don't be driving your grandpa's truck..."

In my grandpa's truck that I turned over.

My brother Ronnie knew his big brother was going to be in major trouble.

Playing football during my junior year.

Skipping school on a Gulf Shores beach. September 1956

SEP 56

With my brother Ronnie and sister Lanette, in front of granddaddy Golden's house.

If you were wonder-
ing what I looked
like with short hair...
a flat top during my
teen years.

My high school FFA Quartet. (L-R) Me, Bud Morris, Gladden Graves, O'Neal Dawson.

My introduction to four-part harmony.

A picture I signed to my sweetheart during my high school senior year.

I Love you!
William

Teenagers in love. Dec. 1956

DEC · 5 6

Wedding Day,
Feb. 16, 1957.
Frogene and
were married i
my parent's
living room.

FEB

The bride
looked stun-
ning. The
groom looked
stunned!

After a successful day of fishing, July 5, 1960.

Visiting with my dad and uncle. Feb. 1960.

In a photo booth, trying to look like Elvis.

Looking for a gospel group to sing with, 196

April 1962

Publicity photos for The Pilots Trio, (L-R) Randy
McDaniel, Hack McCluskey, William, 1961

My professional career was starting to take off! (L-R) Randy McDaniel, William Lee, Hack McCluskey.

On stage with The Pilots Trio, Dec. 1962

Early family photo with Frogene, Craig and Rusty.

The Oak Ridge Boys when I joined the group in 1965. (L-R)
Tommy Fairchild, Little Willie Wynn, William, Smitty Gatlin,
Herman Harper.

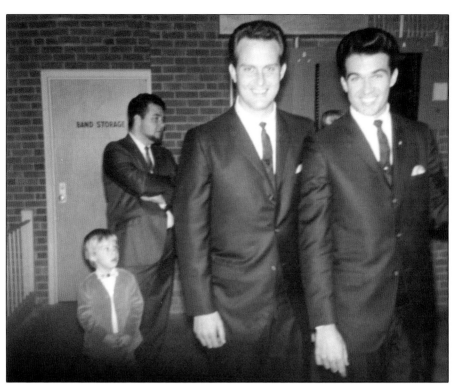

Getting ready to go on stage with Herman Harper.

In the middle of Little Willie Wynn and Tommy Fairchild,
March 1968

Well, if he's an Oak, we've got to pose him by a tree! June, 1968

Traveling in style, by station wagon. Aug 1968.

Yes, music filled our home. (L-R) Rusty, Chris, Craig, my nephew Ron and sister Lanette. 1967

You could always find me, meeting fans by our record rack after our concerts. Oct. 1968

Showing off two of my stage suits. November 1968

OCT · 68

NOV · 68

NOV 68

OAK RIDGE BOYS

First publicity photos of the Oak Ridge Boys after Duane joined the group. He's on the far right.

OAK RIDGE BOYS

The Oak Ridge Boys, 1967. (L-R) William, Tommy Fairchild, Herman Harper, Little Willie Wynn, Duane Allen.

Publicity photo after Noel Fox (far right) joined the group. The photo was taken by the great Nashville photographer Walden Fabry.

OAK RIDGE BOYS

Taking my turn out front, singing lead during the late 60s.

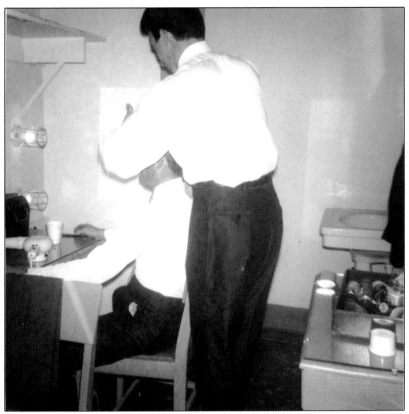

For years, I cut and styled most of the Oaks' hair. Maybe that's why I stopped cutting my own hair!

Belting one out in Fayetteville, NC. Nov. 16, 1969

With Frogene at a gospel awards show.

William Lee Golden, Oct. 1967.
Gary McSpadden took the photo.

Would you buy a Bible from this man? Yes, we promoted and sold them at our concerts!

Giving a Bible to my mother and sister. Duane Allen is on the left.

With my sons Rusty, Chris and Craig.

Playing a little football in our Hendersonville front yard. March, 1969

At Rock City, on one of my few vacations with Rus Craig and Chris.

Promo photo featuring (L-R) Mark Ellerbee, Tommy Fairchild, Don Breland, Willie Wynn, Noel Fox, Duane Allen, William Lee.

Heading to another award show. March, 1970

As our music grew and got more modern, so did our hair.

Still selling albums and signing autographs. May, 1972

Meeting fans by the bus in Mineral Wells, West Virginia.

Picking peaches with a very young Tony Brown.

Family photo with my brother, sister, mother
and father.

Joe Bonsall joins the group. 1974 album featuring the same 4 guys who are still together almost 50 years later!

THE OAKS
Taping Mike Douglas Show, October 1973

Columbia Records

Columbia Records

Joe, Duane, William and Richard perform on the Mike Douglas TV show. Oct. 1973

Frogene and I celebrate the Oaks' Gospel Music Association Album ◄
the Year award. Photo by Michael G. Borum

In the early 70s, I started experiment-ing with a few differ-ent looks.

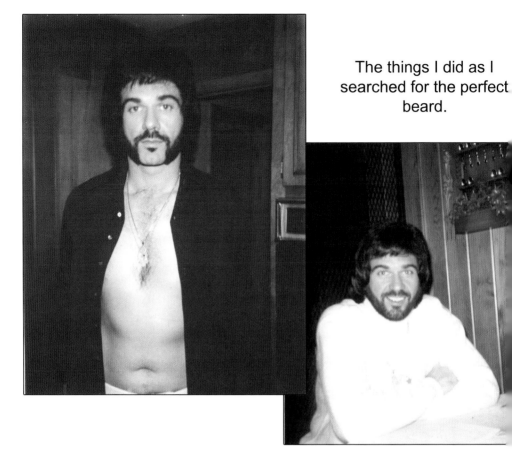

The things I did as I searched for the perfect beard.

Craig, Willi
and Chri
showing o
some of c
favorite 7
fashion. Ja
1976

With Frogene, Christmas, 1979.

Showing Frogene's parents my freshly shaven face. This was the
day I stopped shaving forever.

RUSTY GOLDEN, LEON RUSSELL + WILLIAM LEE GOLDEN - TULSA

© PHOTOGRAPH BY ALAN MESSER ALANMESSER.COM

Visting with my son Rusty and my friend Leon Russell.
Photo by Alan Messer

Signing autographs during our Oak Ridge Boys Fan Fair Open House.

With my parents, April 1979

If you look close, for some reason, I'm wearing two belts. I
guess that was better than two watches!
Photo by Carol Pate Baker

The Oak Ridge Boys. July, 1980. Photo by Carol Pate Baker

With my friends Anne and Paula Pate, July 27, 1980

Carol Pate meeting me for the first time. June, 1980. You can read about the Pate sisters the Fans and Friends Chapter.

Surprising my mother during a rare break from the road.
Photo by Alan Messer

Cheering on
Chris at one of
his high school
football games.

Rusty, William, Craig and Chris all dressed up for Craig's wedding.

My father shows me the baby clothes that he and his triplet brothers wore.

Visiting with one of Rusty's heroes, Elton John. (L-R) Rusty, William Brenda Lee, Elton John, Jo Walker-Meador, Jim Foglesong.

Photo shoot for our
[To]gether album, 1980.
[Ph]oto by Alan Messer

The Oak Ridge Boys,
1980.
Photo by Alan Messer

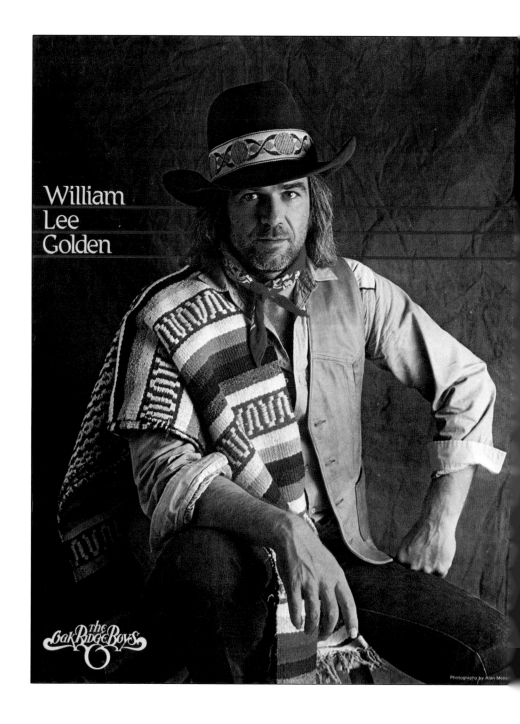

Canvas Poster, 1982. Photo by Alan Messer

TRYING TO LOVE TWO WOMEN

"Trying to love two women is like a ball and chain. Sometimes the pleasure ain't worth the pain."

Frogene was a wonderful wife and a beautiful lady inside and out. She also tried her best to make me beautiful. To keep my hair dark, she colored it at home, and then I would color her hair. We both used the same hair color!

Everything I can say about Frogene is good. She never wanted to be in the spotlight herself. She didn't want to be a star. She just wanted to be there for me. She did anything she could to help me and was so proud of me. Frogene was a hardworking, incredible mother. She supported my dreams and vision. She helped me accomplish the things I wanted to. She was just a wonderful person and a great partner.

So, what caused our problems? I didn't have to look far to find the answer. I saw the cause every time I looked in the mirror.

Everything bad in our marriage came from me, and my weakness as a man. I became friends with my wife's best friend, Patricia. Things started off very innocently, as we'd talk and go to lunch every now and then. We also went to some concerts together. But the relationship evolved into more than friendship, and I wound up having an affair with her.

In all honesty, I have tried to block out a lot of the bad times that I was responsible for. But in an effort to write an open and honest book, I asked Frogene if she remembered how things went down. Little did I know, that she hadn't forgotten a thing. During the last month of her life, she sat down and shared those memories for my book:

"I had a great life with William…until it ended.

My parents and William's parents were great friends. They would all drive up to Nashville together. They all got along very well together.

Long before the Oaks, when William was still farming, he would travel to Arkansas to pick cotton. And as soon as he got off the cotton picker, there would be women chasing after him. He was so good looking, and the ladies loved him. But I didn't believe he would ever look at another woman.

I was close with the entire group of Oak Ridge Boys. All of them had lived with us at some time and I had been a big part of their lives. I never went on the road with the group, because I had a full-time job raising our sons. I loved William so much that I trusted that he was staying true to me while he was on the road. Most people who knew us, wouldn't have believed that he was running around on me. I didn't believe it myself. I didn't think it was possible. But it was.

To make matters much worse, I found out that William was seeing my best friend, someone I loved like a sister.

I was visiting my mom in Brewton, when I got the feeling that William was messing around. I cut my visit short and jumped in our station wagon to head back to Nashville. Rusty was 14 years old and I put him in the back to sleep through the night.

When I got to Nashville just before the sun came up, I drove to the woman's house. Our new Cadillac was in her driveway. My mind started racing. But the Lord spoke to me that night. I heard him loudly say, 'Don't kill that woman. You'll be put in prison and your sons will be without a mother.'

I remembered that I had a key to the Caddy in my purse. So, I parked our station wagon way down the street. I walked to the Cadillac, got in and quietly eased it out of the driveway. I coasted it down the street, picked up Rusty and drove away. A few hours later, William woke up to find his Caddy was gone and all he had was our station wagon…that he had no keys to!

On our way through Hendersonville at 4:00 a.m., a policeman pulled me over. He asked, 'Ma'am, do you have any idea how fast you were driving?' I answered, 'Yes. About 90. But I have a good reason. I just found out that my husband was in bed with my best friend.' The policeman gave me a simple, 'Head on.'

When I got home, I called Duane Allen to tell him what had happened. He came over and begged me not to kill William. A few minutes later, Richard brought William home.

I always felt that William loved me. Even after this incident, he never made me feel that he never loved me.

But my best friend didn't agree. She had fallen in love with my husband and one night she called and announced, 'I don't think William loves you.' I answered, 'I wish you could see how William interacts with me. If you could see us together, you would know he loved me.' She said, 'I wish I could be there.' With that, I instantly came up with a unique plan, saying, 'We can make it happen.'

I know what you are about to read will sound like the craziest thing in the world. It seems like a TV show or something, but this is exactly what happened: The next night, William was coming off the road, and I sent the boys out. William's mistress came over and I put her in the closet! When William walked in, I started asking him about our relationship, and about his relationship with his 'friend.' All during our conversation, she was in the closet, listening to the entire thing.

As William professed his true love for me and assured me that I was his only one, I said, 'Well, there is someone else here who has a different version.' At that moment, the other woman came out of the closet. William's face was something to see. If he hadn't been sitting down, he would have fallen dead! I thought he was going to have a heart attack.

With the three of us now face to face, I put William on the spot. I knew he would tell me the truth…good or bad. He had never lied about anything. Lying was one of the things he really hated. He always told the truth, even if it hurt. And it would hurt today.

When I asked who he loved, William's answer was, 'I love you both.'

As I look back now, William and Patricia really did love each other. After we divorced, they continued to be together for more than five years. But they never got married.

William's unfaithfulness was devastating to me and to our boys. Our happy family was torn apart. But a funny thing happened just a day or so later.

I was at home, crying my eyes out when there was a knock on my door. When I opened it, there stood Johnny Cash…dressed as a woman! The Oaks were playing that night in Waverly, Tennessee and Johnny wanted to take me to the concert. But he didn't want to create a scene, so he was going 'incognito.' I thought, 'He might be in disguise, but I think Johnny Cash in a dress is going to create a scene!' I told him I couldn't go, because I was so upset. It was a surreal moment, as I told him about my husband cheating on me. Johnny was standing there, sad and broken hearted, as he wore a dress…and it wasn't even a black one.

William and I divorced on June 26, 1975. We had been married 18 and half years.

I was mad, but we stayed friends. Since our boys were now in their early teens, William and I attended different school, sports and musical events together. We saw each other at funerals, parties, and graduations, and we also spent our Christmas' together.

Even though we had a bad ending, I still had a wonderful life with William Lee. I always loved and respected him. I wouldn't take anything for the time we had together, and I forgave him long ago for everything he ever did wrong."

— Frogene

When I heard the song "Trying to Love Two Women" for the first time, I said, "That is my story." I had gotten divorced and was trying to live with the girlfriend that I lost my wife over. Yes, I could relate to the lines, "A man can't stock 2 shelves. It's a long hard grind, and it tires your mind."

Trying to love two women can be stressful on your mind, and it can also devastate your bank account. Frogene got 80% of my paycheck. I was OK with that. She deserved whatever she could get. And with what I was making at the time, singing gospel music, 80% wasn't a huge windfall for Frogene.

Our divorce came at the time when the Oak Ridge Boys were really struggling to make ends meet. It seemed the gospel music world was turning its back on us. We couldn't get any bookings, and without concerts, we couldn't sell any records. When I divorced, I was making $250 a week. My child support and alimony were $200 a week. I never complained about that. My kids and my wife needed and deserved that money.

Since the group's finances were so bad, Duane thought he and I should take a $20 a week pay cut, to pay the band members more. He was right. The other guys deserved more money. But that left me with only $30 a week. Have you tried living on $4.25 a day? I wouldn't have survived without the help of my mother and father. When they gave me a used car, I felt embarrassed and guilty that a 35 year-old man had to get help from his parents. I vowed that I would pay them back many times over.

I spent most of 1976, basically living at the Oaks' office. I didn't have a wife, and I had no money. I slept on a couch in our office, and I used the shower and bathroom there for 8 or 9 months. I was at a low point in my life. I had brought all the heartache and financial trouble on myself. But for some reason, I was still full of confidence and optimism. I had nothing but my dream, and I refused to give up. I could still see my vision for the future. And I had no doubt that things were about to change in a big way.

A LITTLE TALK WITH JESUS…
IN A SALOON

Most of our concert dates in 1976 and '77 were with Jimmy Dean. Jimmy was a huge star at the time, and we opened a lot of shows for him. The Oaks were one of the last groups to tour with Jimmy, because a short time later, he got into the sausage business and made himself very rich. He cut back on his touring when he found he could make more money making sausage.

We were on tour with Jimmy when we found out our new single was rocketing up the country music charts. We were finally going to have our first country hit, with a song called "Y'all Come Back Saloon." As the song neared the top of the charts, Jimmy Dean told us that we were outgrowing his show, and that we should go out on our own.

We assured Jimmy that we would stay through all the dates we had been booked for. During that time, just that one country hit song we had really made a big impact. We could all tell that the audience reaction was totally different than it had been just a couple months earlier. Before we left the Jimmy Dean tour, we were proud to say that we had helped him sell quite a few tickets to people who were coming to see the Oak Ridge Boys.

While we had already won 3 Grammy Awards, the 1977 Grammys were extra special, and quite unique. Our new hit "Y'all Come Back Saloon" was nominated for a Grammy for Best Country Performance. We didn't win that award, but The

Oaks did win a Grammy for Best Gospel Performance for "Just a Little Talk with Jesus." It's no wonder many of our fans were confused!

Paul Simon has won a lot more Grammys than The Oaks. Paul Simon had great success as a solo artist, after being a part of the legendary duo Simon and Garfunkel. We had met Paul at an award show and he asked if we'd sing on a new song he was recording. It was called "Slip Slidin' Away." In 1975, he paid for our plane tickets to New York City, so we could record the background vocals for him. He told us exactly how he wanted us to sing, and he loved our harmony. But when the record was finished, there was something about it that he didn't like. Paul decided not to release the song, until he went back into the studio to redo his part. Then he paid for us to fly back a second time to re-do our track. It was finally released in 1977 and was a huge hit for Paul. Our background vocals really stand out on the song, but since our name was not on the record, no one knew it was us. If you have a chance, put on Paul's "Slip Slidin' Away" and listen closely to the background singers. Those guys were getting ready to go places!

"The nearer your destination, the more you're slip slidin' away."

In 1977, the Oak Ridge Boys were near their destination…the Big Time.

THE BIG TIME

Life is such a special gift. I think it's important to experience all you can. Everyone should seek their dreams and go after their goals. We all have different dreams and goals. I saw many of my dreams come true, and the Oak Ridge Boys reached one goal after another as we took the music world by storm.

One key player to our team was a man who you never saw on stage with us. But he was so important that we called him "The 5th Oak Ridge Boy." His name was Ron Chancey, and he was an awesome country music producer. When we made our switch from gospel to country, Ron was with us from the start. He told us, "If we find the right songs, I would like to cut an album on you guys." That album would be our break-through "Y'all Come Back Saloon."

Ron Chancey should get a lot of credit for our success. He found great songs and brought them to us. In addition to the title song, the "Ya'll Come Back Saloon" album also gave us chart toppers "You're the One" and "I'll Be True to You." In just a short time, the album sold more than a half million copies, and was certified gold. Ron also produced our next 3 albums which produced 8 Top Five songs and 2 Number Ones. Every song we released raced up the charts, and we thought we were big stuff. We didn't know what 'big stuff' was. But we were about to find out.

Our career really started to steamroll when we signed on to tour with Kenny Rogers. In the late 70s and early 80s, there was no bigger star in any form of music than Kenny Rogers. When he was at his biggest, playing the largest arenas in the country, the Oak Ridge Boys were playing to the same crowds as we opened his shows.

I was always a fan of Kenny. He was the ultimate professional. I used to buy his records when he was with the First Edition. I loved his "Something's Burning" album, and my favorite song on it was one called "Mama's Waiting." I raised my kids on Kenny Rogers and the First Edition. When Rusty wanted to play drums, I told him to listen to the First Edition, and "Ruby, Don't Take Your Love to Town," so he could get the feel of the rhythm.

Touring with Kenny helped us get comfortable in the setting of a big coliseum. We learned what it took to be a huge act. We also knew how it felt to be the opening act. Kenny always treated us so nice and with such respect, and when we became the headliners, we always wanted to do the same for our opening acts. We had wonderful performers open our shows, including The Bellamy Brothers, The Gatlin Brothers, Janie Fricke, T.G. Sheppard and many more. We always tried to be as nice to our opening acts as Roy Clark, Kenny Rogers and Johnny Cash had been to us.

We did a Christmas tour with Kenny Rogers and Dottie West. Again, we opened the show, and boy was it a spectacular one! Andy Williams was one of the first people to do a big Christmas tour. But Kenny was one of the very first country people to do a Christmas tour. We watched closely as he transformed his usual country concert into a Christmas extravaganza. Then we added our own ideas and started our own Christmas tours. We've now been doing our Christmas shows for over 30 years.

As our career got hotter and hotter, we knew that our days of opening shows for Kenny were coming to an end. With our quickly increasing list of hit songs, we needed more time on stage just to sing them all, and we were confident that we could draw a big crowd with our name at the top of the marquee. Once that decision was made, it seemed like almost overnight, we found ourselves headlining in the same huge arenas that we had just been in when we were Kenny's opening act.

Jim Halsey helped kick our production into high gear, with the best sound and lights in the business. I had been going to see big rock music acts and their stage shows were huge productions with fire and smoke, and they were very entertaining. I told Jim that we should do something similar, and he just ran with it. He got Bob Burwell and Fred Woods who were experts on stage lighting. They brought in computerized laser and lighting systems. Our huge productions also included fog machines and of course, the best sound boards, speakers and equipment available.

I talked with Bruce Lundvall, who was one of the head guys at Columbia Records in New York. I told him that I had an idea for a logo for the group, that we could use for a big backdrop during our concerts. Bruce had the man who designed the logo for the group 'Chicago' make one for us. The finished product was a work of art that we also used on our stationery, ads and merchandise.

We had three tour buses and three semis to carry everything and everyone on our growing crew. It took a lot of money to pay for our team, and as our booking price rose, we wanted to give the audience the most impressive show we possibly could. When the Oak Ridge Boys tour buses and semis rolled in, it sometimes looked like the circus had come to town. At times we felt like carnies. Our life was very similar to carnival workers who move from one city to another, set up in the day and tear down overnight. Many people think our lives are quite glamorous, but if you've ever been backstage at a circus, you'll find there is not a whole lot of glamour. As a matter of fact, you have to watch out where you step!

As we tried to keep up with our hectic pace, members of my family worried that I would get swept up in the trappings that come with fame and fortune. My sister Lanette was one who prayed for me daily. As I was writing this book, she shared some of the feelings she had during those years:

"I was always proud of William, before and after he got 'famous.' When things were going so fast for the Oak Ridge Boys, I got a little worried about him. I was afraid of all the temptations that were coming his way. But I had faith that mother's and daddy's prayers would protect him and would get him back on track if he went down the wrong road.

I made sure I was at every Oak Ridge Boys concert when they came anywhere near Brewton. It made me proud as I watched the crowd go crazy for my brother. I've always bragged on William. One day, I was at Gayfer's Department Store in Pensacola and I heard William singing, 'Thank God for Kids' over the speakers. I smiled and said out loud, 'Yes, that's my brother.'

William has a big heart. He loved, appreciated, and honored his parents. He still honors them today, long after they passed. He is fair and he's sincere. All the fans love him. They love him because he takes time with them. He gets out of the bus and talks to his fans. He has done that for decade after decade. William has been a very good brother, and I am proud to be his sister."

— Lanette Lowery

During an event in Tulsa, Oklahoma, in 1978, I met a man who would become one of my closest friends. His name was

Alan Messer. Alan was an amazing photographer who has led a truly incredible life.

When he was 16 years old, Alan went to work for Dezo Hoffman, who took all the famous album cover shots and publicity photos for The Beatles. Alan became Dezo's assistant, and when he was still a teenager, Alan ended up doing his own photo shoots with The Beatles, Jimi Hendrix, The Rolling Stones and Jim Morrison and the Doors.

Alan moved to Nashville in the late 1970s, and he became a legendary country music photographer. He went on to take thousands of photos of the Oaks and even more of just me. Alan and I became instant friends and we have enjoyed each other's company over thousands of miles. Alan took the photo that's on the cover of this book. I thank him for sharing his talent and friendship with me over so many years. Here are a few of Alan's memories of our time together:

> "Behind the beard is my friend, Bill. We first met in Tulsa, Oklahoma in 1978 at a reception held by Jim Halsey. In April of 1977, the Oak Ridge Boys manager had asked me to take some pictures of the band at the International Country Music Festival at Wembley Arena, England. Those photographs and some of Don Williams, also Halsey's artist, helped pave my way into Nashville.
>
> I've taken thousands of photographs of William Lee Golden and of the Oak Ridge Boys. I enjoyed working with the Oak Ridge Boys on some of their tour books, albums and publicity. Bill (as I call him) also hired me to photograph some of his personal projects and promotions. Golden (as his brother Oaks call him) is a creative artist, whose art extends past his baritone four-part harmony to his individual recordings, to his paintbrush, to his cameras and to his stories. I shot and art directed his first fan poster in 1982, his solo album, American Vagabond and

several of his son's projects: The Goldens, Golden Speer and Cedar Creek.

I have witnessed and photographed four decades of the Golden family (so far). I have seen that beard sprout and grow with many photo sessions, from a scruffy GQ look, which influenced the look of the Oak Ridge Boys 1980 "Together" album tour, his mid 80's Mountain Man era (which was fun and visually exciting to photograph), though to present time. We made the book cover photograph during Bill's eightieth birthday party at his home, Golden Era, on January 12th, 2019.

Our friendship is based on a mutual respect of each other and our careers, a friendship that has endured four decades. William Lee Golden comes from a time and a family where the spoken word is a bond. When hard work was daily life.

One of my memorable photo sessions with Golden wasn't when I was taking his photograph. One night, around midnight, I get a phone call from Tanya Tucker. She asked if she could come over to my studio and take some pictures. "NOW?" I responded, "Okay come on." I phoned Bill, who got there at about 2 am as we were in full photo swing. My assistant and I set up my studio lights in the bathroom to photograph Tanya in my shower, wearing a T-shirt and full makeup. When Bill arrived, I asked him to stand on the toilet, holding a waterbed hose which mixed the water temperature. He sprayed Tanya with the water, and I got a classic Tanya Tucker photograph.

November 2, 2019 was William Lee's homecoming event in Brewton, which also aligned with Alabama's bicentennial. He was on a tight schedule performing with the Oak Ridge Boys, so he chartered a private plane so he could celebrate his homecoming and be back in time to be on stage that same night! His plane landed at the same airfield that had been the scene of his jam-packed Harvest Jam festival back in 1981. During the homecoming, I did a slide show presentation encompassing a cross section of photographs I've taken of him over the years, while Golden told stories. Some of those stories and pictures are in this book.

Behind the beard is an encompassing ever-present smile and a man of enduring vitality and energy."

— Alan Messer

Alan mentioned our photoshoot with Tanya Tucker. Tanya is a trooper, and she was always fun. She's always been a hard worker ever since she was a little girl. She had drive and determination to go with her great talent. She is so deserving of the comeback and success she's had in recent years.

The Oak Ridge Boys loved singing, and performing in front of sold-out arenas was an awesome feeling. It brought all of us so much joy to be able to share our music with millions of people around the country. There were many months when we were gone 25 days. We were workhorses. We were never home, and our heavy touring schedule took us away from our families who we loved so much. During our heyday, our lives were in a spin, with people pulling at us from every side.

On March 5, 1978, The Oak Ridge Boys played to more than 60, 000 people at the Silverdome in Pontiac, Michigan. The show was billed as "The World's Largest Indoor Country Music Show." It was hosted by Kenny Rogers and Dottie West. Grand Ole Opry legends Roy Acuff, Bill Monroe and Minnie Pearl were also on the show with us. It was pretty amazing listening backstage as 60, 000 people yelled "How-Dee!" with Minnie Pearl.

You would have thought that I was contented to be singing to 60, 000 adoring fans. But I wasn't. I knew we had still not reached our peak. In the summer of 1979, in an interview with People magazine, I said, "Inevitably, our music will cross all borders and labels. Someday, we're gonna run across something that everybody will like at the same time, and when that happens, we'll have it made." I could see exactly how it would happen, and the time was ticking down…2 years and counting…until "Elvira".

In the meantime, we continued to play to big audiences. Large crowds always turned out for the "Jamboree in the Hills" in Wheeling, West Virginia. Each year, they had a star-studded lineup and we were at the top of the bill, as we played to 50, 000 fans. The big festivals were some of the greatest fun times I ever had. When you sing to 50, 000 people, who can like you or not like you, it's kind of like walking a tightrope. It has that same kind of petrifying fear the first time you step out there. But when those 50, 000 fans are singing along with every word and screaming louder than your stage monitors, there is no better feeling in the world.

The "Big Valley Jamboree" in Canada and "Country Jam USA" in Wisconsin are two similar events. They are two of my favorites that we've played numerous times. We played the Mervyn Conn festival in Europe, that featured country music acts. Slim Whitman was a huge star there, and Don Williams and Boxcar Willie were superstars in Europe, lots bigger than they were in the U.S.

We had traveled to Europe several times in the early days of our country music career. Those tours were never big financial successes. It costs so much to get there and then we had to rent our buses and equipment. We didn't make a lot of money, but we were spreading our music and name around the world. There are still a lot of places I would like to play that we've never been to. One of those is Australia. I'd like to perform there and there are quite a few countries I think would be fun to visit.

It's not easy going from being on stage and having 10, 000 to 50, 000 people applauding and screaming your name to go to the bus and try to go to sleep. I usually stayed up all night, even in our gospel music days. Noel Fox, our gospel bass singer, and I would stay up all night, talking. Noel would finally say, "What are we doing up at 3:00 am?" I'd answer, "We're both afraid we're gonna miss something."

When you do 150 to 250 concerts a year for more than 50 years, there are bound to be occasional challenges that come up. Weather related issues would top that list. We've performed in every kind of weather. We've played some hot ones, with the temperature over 100 degrees. Ten minutes into the show, we would be sweating so much that you could call us The Soaked Ridge Boys. To prepare for that situation, I began walking outside in the middle of the day. I walked a few miles each day, when the sun was at its hottest, and that training gave me the confidence that I could handle a two hour show in any conditions.

In addition to my walking, I also try to do at least 125 sit-ups every day. I do 5 sets of 25, usually in my hotel room a few hours before our concert. The sit-ups help my lung capacity and breathing. A few of our songs can wear you out and have you gasping for breath before they're over. One of those is one I sing lead on called, "I Wish You Could Have Turned My Head." The song is in a strange key and you have to hold your notes way up there. It's a strain and by the end I'm looking for breath.

But some things, you just can't prepare for. One was a May concert in the middle of an Iowa cornfield. When they turned our stage lights on, the mayflies came at us. Those flies came from everywhere. Our huge spotlights attracted flies from many miles away. As we sang, the flies were getting down in our shirts, and as we performed, we started stepping on them. There were hundreds of smashed bugs, so many that the stage floor started getting slick! We all finally decided that we should just stand still and sing. People probably wondered why Joe wasn't running and jumping all over the stage like he normally did, but he didn't want to fall down in a pile of smashed bug guts!

We played the Kansas State Fair one time and the wind was so strong that I had to keep holding onto my cowboy hat. My beard and hair were blowing sideways. We always watch the local weather forecast and keep an eye on the radar. We've had to cut a few shows short when a storm blows in out of nowhere. But it has to get pretty dangerous for that to happen. We've done much more Singin' in the Rain than Gene Kelly ever thought of doing.

While the Oaks were reaching one new goal after another, I came up with a new, personal goal to go after. I had always dreamed of promoting a huge event in my hometown of Brewton, Alabama. I wanted to model it after the "Volunteer Jams" that Charlie Daniels had hosted. When the Oak Ridge Boys played his Jam, I told Charlie about my dream. He smiled his big smile and said, "Go for it, son! Get it done." He had all the faith in the world that I could put on a successful event.

I had promoted many Oak Ridge Boys concerts back in our gospel music days, and also in the early days of our country career. I always enjoyed promoting shows, and when a good promoter booked us for a show, I liked to talk to them to get their advice and tips for concert promotion. I also met some promoters who didn't know what they were doing. They booked us and thought just because they had a name act, that people would show up without any promotion.

But Jim Fitzgerald was one of the best promoters in the business. He was a long-time friend who had successfully put on the World's Largest Country Indoor Country Music Show a couple years earlier. Jim came to Brewton and gave me his advice on how I could throw the biggest party my hometown had ever seen.

The last time I had performed in Brewton, I was part of a struggling gospel music act. Now, the same group, The Oak Ridge Boys were one of the hottest things going in any form of music. I started putting together the show I would call "Harvest Jam" right when we were starting to have our greatest success. And before the event was held, we would release a little song called "Elvira." Brewton, Alabama didn't know what was about to hit it.

While I started booking the talent for Harvest Jam in 1980, the show itself was set for October 10, 1981. Since I was busy on the road with the Oaks, who were working non-stop at the time, I hired a friend named Ely Ball to help me with a lot of behind-the-scenes details. Ely was a college student in Minneapolis, and he promoted concerts while he was in college. When he brought the Oak Ridge Boys into the big arena in Minneapolis, I asked him to help me with my Harvest Jam.

I brought in my lawyer Bill Carter, to be in charge of crowd security. That turned out to be one of the biggest and most important jobs. But I knew Bill was up to the task, since he had been a Secret Service agent under Presidents Kennedy and Johnson. Bill hired 50 off-duty Mobile police officers to provide security for the Harvest Jam. I also hired Ben Ferrell and Reggie Churchwell. Reggie helped promote the event, by visiting every radio station and newspaper office from Birmingham to northern Florida.

Since I was in charge of booking all the acts, I wanted entertainers who would draw a crowd, but I also wanted to have people who I liked and enjoyed working with. Of course, I booked the Oak Ridge Boys, and I paid them their full price. I also booked the man who had first told me I could put on such an event, Charlie Daniels and his Charlie Daniels Band. I added a new band that was just catching on called Alabama, and since I had a major crush on Sylvia, I signed her onto the show.

My choices of artists could not have worked out better. Between the time I booked them, at fairly inexpensive prices, Charlie Daniels, Alabama and Sylvia all had numerous major hits. Charlie was at his peak, with everyone singing along to "The Devil Went Down to Georgia", Sylvia was getting real hot as she prepared to release her mega-hit "Nobody," and Alabama had 5 number one songs during that time! And just after I had booked the Oak Ridge Boys, we released "Elvira" and we took over the entire world. The Oaks were at their very hottest and I was bringing them to my (very little) hometown.

To pay for all those acts, I had been saving all the money I was making from my Oaks job. I knew being a concert promoter was a risky business. You could make a lot of money, and you could also lose every penny you had. While I didn't gamble in the Las Vegas casinos, I didn't mind taking a huge gamble on something I knew…and I knew country music.

In 1981, Brewton had a population of less than 7, 000 people. The only place with a large enough area for my dream concert was the Brewton airport. We had three miles of space out there that would be more than enough for our parking needs, and we set up the huge stage on the airstrip. As the day of the concert neared, I worried that no one would show up. If we didn't get a crowd, I would lose a lot of money.

I shouldn't have worried. 55, 000 people. Yep. 55, 000 people showed up…in a town of less than 7, 000!

You have never seen a traffic jam like the one in Brewton, Alabama that day. The people just kept coming. There was a 10 mile line of cars, trying to get in. That was one problem I hadn't planned on. We actually sold 40, 000 tickets. But it took so long to get people in, that the other 15, 000 finally tore down the fences in the back, and they just poured in without buying a ticket. I didn't mind though. I know they would have paid, if they could have just gotten up to the main gate. And we sold more than enough to make a lot of money.

During the show, I sang The Beatles' song "Long and Winding Road." As I sang, I thought of the long and winding road that had taken me out of Brewton, around the world and now back to where I began.

Everyone made a profit, and everybody had a great time. Everyone I guess, except my dad, who I brought out on stage during our finale. At the time, I was wearing a pair of cut-off jean shorts. Dad looked out over the sea of 55, 000 people and then looked at my shorts. His only words to me were, "Son, why don't you get some britches on."

In 1982, the popular ABC network show "20/20" wanted to do a long feature piece on the Oak Ridge Boys. The man in charge of the "20/20" story was a producer named Jeff Panzer. I had met Jeff a year earlier, when he did a similar piece on the country group Alabama. Little did I know at that first meeting, that Jeff would become my very best friend. Jeff was one of the first people I told about this book. I also asked him to share some of his memories of the first years of our friendship:

> "I met William Lee through a mutual friend, Kay Shaw West. I was producing a story on the group Alabama, and Kay was doing publicity for Alabama's record label, RCA.
>
> While I was in Nashville, Kay told me there was someone I needed to meet. Kay said, 'I have a friend and you are going to love him. His name is William Lee Golden.' I was from the big city, and wasn't really into country music. I didn't know much about The Oak Ridge Boys. I was also focused on getting my piece done on Alabama, but Kay insisted on taking me out to William's home.

When we pulled in, the front lawn looked like a huge concert was happening. There was loud music, and people inside and outside the house. People were everywhere. We went downstairs and I saw William sitting on a couch, visiting with some of his guests. Kay introduced us and within the first 15 minutes of us meeting, William had me hypnotized. When I was talking with him, he stared right at me and listened to every word I said.

William was like a gentle giant, with long flowing hair, a big beard and eyes that just mesmerized you. During our visit, I found he was into rock and roll, in addition to country music. He was a wealth of knowledge about all different types of music.

When I left, I knew why Kay thought I should meet this guy. I knew instantly that something special had just happened in my life. I felt that I had really connected with William on a number of levels. That connection has not only remained, but has grown over the last four decades. Through the good and bad that life has offered us, William has stood by me, like I stood by him.

Maybe it is true that 'opposites attract.' William and I are so different in our upbringings and where we came from. He is from a farm in southern Alabama and I'm a Jewish guy from Long Island. But we somehow connected emotionally, mentally, and spiritually. There was a common bond that was made that first meeting, and we have that bond to this day. No matter what, William knows that if he needs me, I will come runnin', and vice versa.

The secret to our friendship is loyalty. We know we can be truthful and honest with each other. William is a very straightforward type of guy. He's laid back and people think because he talks slow with his Brewton, Alabama accent, that he's not smart. But he is a very deep, sharp man. He is also a trendsetter in every sense of the word, whether that is fashion, style, or music.

William is a very giving man. I hope that I can give back half as much as he has given me. He has such a huge heart. He gives love to everyone he meets. He gives his time for his fans. He is so accessible, and so down to earth. When he signs autographs, he gives each person as much time as they want.

William has had a life of ups and downs, as you'll find out in these pages. Some of the ups were so high, back in the 1980s, as they filled the hugest arenas as headliners. But then he hit the lowest of lows, when his phone wasn't ringing anymore. It was then that he found out who his friends really were.

When he told me he was writing this book, I laughed and asked, 'Is this what you really want to do?' But I think it is really appropriate. He is one of the most underated people in the music world. William was brought up believing in faith, family, friends, and music. He was raised on those values. That's what his life has always been about and that's what his life still is and will always be. William has taught me so much about life. I hope he can say the same about me.

To have the fortune of being a friend of someone who is the caliber of a human being that William is, I am one of the most fortunate people in the world. I am blessed to have him in my life. I know that no matter what, I have a friend who will be there for me. He is a special, special man who has a whole lot of love in his heart for everyone he touches, and that is a very unique quality to have."

— Jeff Panzer

Jeff did a wonderful TV story on us for "20/20." It was an 18-minute mini-documentary that really helped introduce us to many households that hadn't heard of us before. I wanted to make sure my parents saw the story, so I asked Jeff to go with me to my childhood home in Alabama.

It might be hard for people to believe, but in 1982, my mom and dad did not own a television. They had never had one! When I was growing up, we were too poor to afford one, and if I wanted to see a TV show, I had to go to my cousin's house, a quarter mile down the road. Other than that, we didn't watch TV, and we never went to the movies. And even when dad started making more money, having a TV was just not very high up on his priority list. It wasn't on his list at all!

My parents would hear from their friends that the Oak Ridge Boys had been on TV, but mom and dad never saw us. So, Jeff and I took the Oak Ridge Boys' tour bus from Nashville to Brewton, and we brought my parent's the first television they ever had. It was a big, heavy, color TV. Jeff hooked it up and showed them how to operate it.

We wanted to show them the "20/20" piece, but we didn't have a video cassette player for the TV. Luckily, the bus had a state-of-the-art video system, so we took dad out to the bus. We played the feature story for my father, and I couldn't wait to see his reaction when he saw exactly how popular his son and the Oak Ridge Boys had become.

The video included a short clip of reporter John Stossel interviewing me in front of my teepee. I had just started my "Mountain Man" look, and I wore buckskin pants and no shirt for the interview.

Dad watched the entire piece in total quiet, and when it ended, I expected him to say, 'William, you've really made good. We're proud of you.' But instead, he said, 'Son, why didn't you put on a shirt? The next time you're on TV, you need to get some clothes on.' That was his one and only comment.

My father eventually did start watching the news on his new TV. But as soon as it was over, he would turn the TV off. He didn't want it to "waste electricity." My parents might not have been watching, but millions of other people were tuned in when The Nashville Network went on the air. TNN asked us to host a "Live From Las Vegas" weekly series.

Sherman Halsey, the son of our manager Jim Halsey, directed the "Live From Las Vegas" shows. Sherman also directed numerous music videos for us and all the "Feed the Children" specials we did. Being the son of Jim Halsey could have been a very intimidating thing, but Sherman made his own mark in Music City, as he became one of the most talented directors in the country. Sherman passed away in 2013, at the too-young age of just 56. He was a wonderful man.

One of Richard Sterban's friends was our wardrobe stylist for the "Live From Las Vegas" series. They wanted us all to look our very best, but I was more into buckskins and cowboy hats. I was a little uncomfortable in some of the more stylish designer clothes they put me in, but I went along with it.

When it came to stage clothes, the Oak Ridge Boys were always one of the most stylish acts going. We seemed to be just a little bit ahead of our time...for good and bad. In our gospel music days, we all wore matching outfits. All the gospel acts did that. I think it kind of helped our fans identify us, like professional ball players, you could tell which team we were on by our uniforms. It also helped us keep track of each other when we played those all-night gospel sings with a lot of other acts.

I look back at some of those clothes and have to laugh. One outfit was a sweater and pants that were made out of the same type of material. They both had a pattern that looked like a snake. Why would I wear that on a gospel show?! I wouldn't dream of wearing that today, and I can't believe I wore it out in public and on stage.

I was into fashion, but times were changing, and I was going to a lot of pop and rock music shows. I noticed that the pop and rock and roll bands had gotten away from dressing alike, like they did in the '60s. But country music always seemed to embrace change much more slowly. In country, if a group didn't have identical wardrobes, it was looked on as a kind of rebellion.

The Statler Brothers, who usually swept the country music award shows, wore matching suits through most of their career. I think a lot of radio DJs and many fans looked at the Statlers and Oak Ridge Boys as major competitors. But that was never the case to me. Of course, we were both quartets, but we were totally different, and I thought there was more than enough room on country radio, the charts and in the concert halls for both of us.

But I understood the comparisons between the two groups. In their career, the Statler Brothers racked up 33 Top Ten songs. The Oak Ridge Boys had 34 Top Tens. While the Oaks won our fair share of awards, the Statlers won a lot more than we did. They had won the Country Music Association Vocal Group of the Year Award six years in a row. But on October 9, 1978, we finally won that award at the 12th annual CMAs. During our acceptance speech, we thanked Johnny Cash for believing in us when no one else did.

Of course, Johnny had also supported the Statlers, and he had them as part of his show before they had any hits at all. But now the hits were coming for the Statlers and the Oaks. Most of the new Statler hit songs were coming thanks to their newest member, Jimmy Fortune. When Jimmy joined them, he brought along his amazing songwriting and even more impressive voice. He made them more up-to-date and gave them so many classic hits. I love Jimmy and I think he helped extend the Statlers' career at least two decades. But the Oaks had something the Statlers didn't…our live shows. When it came to our concerts, both groups always sold out almost everywhere they played. But honestly, I thought our shows were much more high energy than theirs.

When the Statler Brothers retired, Jimmy Fortune was still quite young, and he wanted to continue performing. So, we invited him to be our opening act on quite a few shows. He was very nervous to be out there on his own after being in a group for so many years, but he did just great, and he fit right in on our show. It's kind of ironic that all our fans really loved Jimmy, but quite a few of the old Statler Brother fans didn't like seeing him on our show. They still saw the two groups as competitors. We weren't.

One thing that set the Oak Ridge Boys apart from any other group, was the fact that all four of the Oaks, Richard, Joe, Duane and I have individually sung lead on number one songs. Richard sang lead on "Dream On." Of course, he also had the signature licks on "Elvira" with his "Oom Poppa Mau-Mau." Then, he had the "Ba-Ba-Ba-Ba" on "Bobbie Sue."

Duane has the lead on "Ya'll Come Back Saloon," "I'll Be True to You," and many more. Joe leads on "I Guess It Never Hurts to Hurt Sometime" and "Love Song," and I take the main mic on "Tryin' to Love Two Women," "Thank God for Kids" and "I Wish You Could Have Turned My Head, and Left My Heart Alone."

We all cheered on each other when the other person had the lead on a song. I had pushed for that from the beginning. I wanted each member to take turns in the spotlight. That's what we always did in gospel music and I thought it would also work in country music. It helped keep our music fresh and all our songs sounded different, because each new radio single had a different guy singing.

I was never jealous of my partners. I wanted to build them all up and get each one out front. I wanted us all to do good, and I never tried to hog the spotlight. Duane, Joe and Richard were also team players. None of them wanted to be the one and only star of the show. We all knew that if one of the others was singing lead on a song and it went to number one, we all got paid the same money and each of us got his own gold or platinum record.

There are many things that can distract you from your goals and dreams. If you don't keep your focus, they can pull you away from what you are doing. At the end of the day (and it usually is at the end of our day) when it's time to get up on stage, you've got to be ready to sing. You've got to be on time and ready to give it everything you've got. Each one of the Oak Ridge Boys have done that every night, for our entire career.

I suppose if you are a solo act, you might be able to get away with having a big ego. If you get a big head and are full of yourself, it probably won't make you any friends, but your career could still survive. But it's a different matter when you are part of a group. When you're in a group, it's important that everyone sets their egos outside the door when you go to perform. I look at the other guys in the Oak Ridge Boys and I see that everybody is sacrificing to be there. Everyone else has a song to sing, and if you're part of a group, you've got to be a team player.

We all wanted our group to be around for the long term, and it takes a team effort for that to happen. In 1980, we hired one of our greatest team players. When Ronnie Fairchild joined us on keyboards, he was carrying on his family tradition. His dad Tommy had played for the Oak Ridge Boys from the late '50s to early '70s. But his son Ronnie made Tommy's long run with us seem like a cup of coffee. Ronnie has now been with the Oaks for over 40 years!

Every time we went into the studio, we all remembered what Jim Halsey had told us when we first met. "You guys are just 3 minutes away from being a household name." All we needed was a hit record that crossed all musical borders. It sounded easy, but something like that happened very rarely, especially in country music.

But in 1981, it happened. We recorded a 3-minute song called "Elvira." Dallas Frazier had written the song 16 years earlier. A few people had recorded the song over those years, including Kenny Rogers and Charlie Rich, but no one had ever had a hit with it.

When we were in the studio recording "Elvira," we knew it had a good time feel. Everyone was into it and it was a fun day, but none of us had any idea that the song would become the mega-hit of our career.

We found out that we had something magical the first time we sang the song on stage. The show was in Spokane, Washington. "Elvira" hadn't been released to radio yet, and we just put it in the middle of our concert. At the end of the song, the place went wild. And they kept applauding...so much that we started singing the song again. That was something we had never, ever done before. At the end of our second version, the crowd continued to cheer. They just went crazy. So, we sang it again for the third time! We finally had to move on and do the rest of the show, but it was all a let-down after that song.

When "Elvira" was released to radio, it went straight to number one. Then it crossed over into pop music, and rocketed right to the top of the pop charts. All the rock music stations started playing it, and millions of people were singing along to Richard Sterban's low note "Oom Poppa Mau-Mau." Every TV show and every concert promoter in America wanted to book the Oak Ridge Boys. "Elvira" became the biggest song and single ever sold in country music at that point.

Just like Jim Halsey had told us...a simple 3-minute song had turned us into superstars and household names. Whether you were a country fan or not, you knew the name "The Oak

Ridge Boys." Many people who were just learning our name thought "Elvira" was our first song! But we had enjoyed a dozen big hits before we ever recorded "Elvira."

People often ask us "Who was the real Elvira?" As a coincidence, one of the more influential women in my hometown of Brewton, Alabama was Elvira McMillan. Her family really helped build Brewton. Everyone in town called her Miss Elvira, and believe it or not, her mother was named Elvira, her daughter was named Elvira and her granddaughter was named Elvira! So of course, when the song hit, their whole family thought it was about them, and they just loved it. But the man who wrote the song, Dallas Frazier, had never met the McMillan Elviras.

"Elvira" won the 1981 Grammy Award for Best Country Performance. It also won the Academy of Country Music Song of the Year and Country Music Association Song of the Year awards. It sold over 5 million records. But the song was so popular that it gave us some challenges when it came to our live performances. Once the song became such a huge hit, of course we wanted to save it for last in our concerts. But every single show, we always had people screaming out during the show, "Sing Elvira!" We'd be one song into the show, and someone would yell, "Do Elvira!" Of course, there was no way we were not going to sing it, but they wanted it right then, early in the show. Finally, Joe came up with the line that he told them every night, "We will sing Elvira in a little while, but when we start that song, our driver starts the bus. He knows it's time to go when he hears Elvira."

Once "Elvira" finally started to fall from number one, we released "Fancy Free." It was a great follow-up and went right to number one. Our next release was the title track of our brand new album, and when it comes to big hits, it would give "Elvira" a run for its money. "Bobbie Sue" went to the top of the country and pop music charts, and once again, people around the country were singing to Richard's low note 'Ba-Ba, Ba-Ba...Bobbie Sue.'

Later that year, we released our first Christmas album, and our record label chose one song to release just before Christmas of 1982. It was a song that Eddy Raven had written and recorded ten years earlier. Eddy had wanted to release it as a single, but his record company didn't like it. Eddy and I became great friends and I asked him to share his thoughts on how he came to write such a special song:

> "I held the pen as I wrote 'Thank God for Kids,' but I always felt that there was a higher power that directed my words.
>
> The process of writing it began when I was coming back from a concert in South Carolina. Johnny Duncan was riding back to Nashville with us, and we stopped at a rest area in the Smokies. I saw a group of children sliding down a hill and I remarked to Johnny, 'I used to have energy like that...Thank God for Kids.' Johnny said, 'That's a hit song. You need to write that.' When I got back in our vehicle, I wrote the title 'Thank God for Kids' on a brown grocery bag.
>
> After I got home, I was sitting at my desk, when my 3-year-old son Ryan came in with his little toy guitar. He asked, 'What are you doing Daddy?' I said, 'Tryin' to write a song.' Ryan pulled up a chair and said, 'I'll help you.' But just as we started, he heard Sesame Street on TV in the other room, and he ran off. As I watched him, I saw that paper bag with the title 'Thank God for Kids' on it. Fifteen minutes later, I had written that song. It was magic
>
> Being the oldest of ten children, I could relate to kids. When I played it for my producer Don Gant, he said, 'That's the best song you will ever write.' Then we

played my demo of the song for Wesley Rose at Acuff-Rose Music. When Wesley heard it, he said, 'You will never write another song as great as that one is.'

But my record label didn't think country fans wanted to hear a song about kids. In 1976, they put it out as a B-Side to a song called 'Curse of A Woman,' and it went nowhere. Six long years later, I got word that the Oak Ridge Boys were going to record my song. And when I heard the Oak's version of the song, I thought, 'Well, it's not my song anymore. That's William's song now.'

After it became such a big hit for the Oaks, I always made sure to do it in my own concerts. I'd explain that I was the guy who wrote the song. One night, a woman came up to me after the show and said, 'You did a really good job singing that song...but you're no William Lee Golden.'

William and I have always had a lot of respect for each other, and 'Thank God for Kids' has been the keystone for my career. It's been recorded so many times, by so many people, including John Rich and Kenny Chesney. But it still belongs to William Lee.

I think the world of all the Oaks. They are just a wonderful group of guys. They aren't making groups like the Oak Ridge Boys anymore. And I thank God for William Lee Golden."

– Eddy Raven

I sang lead on our version of "Thank God for Kids," and we watched as it headed up the charts. We thought it would start falling when Christmas came and went, but instead, it continued climbing. It went right into the new year, and DJs continued to play it, and during the first week of February it hit number 3.

The first time I sang "Thank God for Kids" in concert was when we were filming an HBO special in 1982. We were at the big arena in Pine Bluff, Arkansas. Charlie Daniels shared the bill with us, and Rosanne Cash opened the show. We did the TV special that fall, just before our Christmas album was finished, and the show producer wanted us to perform the song that night.

When I sang the song for the first time, in front of a live audience, I was shy and timid. I thought, "This crowd is rowdy and wants to boogie, and here I am getting ready to do this slow, simple song." I figured a lot of the crowd wasn't even married and they were hoping I would get it over with as soon as possible. But we performed it and at the end of the song, it got a huge response.

"Thank God for Kids" became much more than just a Christmas song. It is a year-round song. When I first recorded "Thank God for Kids," I thought it told a great story, but I had no idea it would become such a big hit. But it just struck a chord with people, and it has become my signature song. A month after it was released, I became a grandfather, so when we sang it in concert, I started ending it with the tag, "And thank God for grandkids too," and the crowd always goes wild.

"Thank God for Kids" is still one of our most popular songs. It has also helped raise money for a lot of children organizations and charitable groups, including the Shriners, that have used it for their campaigns.

Ron Chancey got to know each of our capabilities and each one's strengths and weaknesses as vocalists. He found the Randy Van Warmer song "I Guess It Never Hurts to Hurt Sometimes" and thought it would be perfect for Joe to sing. When we went into the studio to record it, Joe started singing kind of like the Bee Gees, and Ron said, "That's it!" Joe used that falsetto voice, and it became a huge hit.

I sang lead on quite a few of our big hits. "I Wish You Could Have Turned My Head and Left My Heart Alone" was written by Sonny Throckmorton, but I could really relate to it. And of course, "Trying To Love Two Women" was kind of my theme song for a while.

One song I really love is "Ozark Mountain Jubilee." Roger Murrah and Scott Anders wrote it. It takes me back to my homeplace in Alabama, every time I perform it.

"Touch a Hand, Make a Friend" was our 13th number one song. When we sang it in concert, all four of us would go down to the front of the stage and even out into the audience and shake hands with as many people as we could. Unfortunately, we had to cut back on that personal touch when the Covid 19 pandemic came along.

One of the most special Christmas songs I sing lead on is "Mary, Did You Know?" Buddy Greene wrote the music, and comedian Mark Lowry wrote the lyrics that will outlive him. It's a serious song and delicate question. I love singing it and Roger Eaton's guitar work is just stellar on that song.

I truly enjoy all our songs, and I never get tired of singing "Elvira," "Bobbie Sue" or any of our hits. Even if I did get burnt out on a song, on stage I would still sing it with the same feeling as I always did. We're not up there to please ourselves. The fans buy the tickets, and you need to sing the songs they want to hear.

One of the things that made the Oak Ridge Boys such a force on stage was our "Mighty Oaks Band." We had, and still have, some incredible musicians. In 1981, I pushed us to hire a talented young man named Steve Sanders. Steve had started singing gospel music when he was just 5 years old. He went by "Little Stevie" and "Singin' Steve" as he worked with the Florida Boys and Happy Goodman Family, and by the time he was 12, he was quite popular.

By 1981, Steve's child-star days were long behind him. But I knew that he was still a very talented guy. I thought he would be a perfect rhythm guitar player for the Oak's band. I could see his talent, but I could also see that his current look that included real long hair and a long beard, wouldn't fly with the more conservative group members or fans. I said, "Steve, we need to clean you up." I took him to a high-end hair stylist who gave Steve a new haircut and beard style. Steve looked great for his first photo shoot for the Boys Band. Ironically, I started letting my hair and beard grow right after that!

Steve Sanders was one of many wayward souls who stayed at my house. He lived there off and on for a couple years as he played for us. He was going through some difficult times in his marriage (something I could relate to) I told him he was welcome anytime, and he came and hung out with me quite a bit.

If you've attended one of our concerts, you might have heard me exclaim, "I feel like singin' all night!" That became a line I said almost every night. I said it because that's exactly how I felt. I love to sing and when the crowd is into it, I would sing for 3 or 4 hours if they would let me. We had spent all night driving across the country, then we waited all day to perform, so when I finally got up on stage, I really did feel like singing all night. I thought longer shows also gave the fans their money's worth. I'd go see rock acts like Bruce Springsteen and he would do a minimum of 3 hours. His show just blew away a lot of the country acts I saw who were doing a 45 minute or one hour concert.

I always thought the rock acts gave much more memorable concerts than country artists. I've gone to a lot of shows and I think I've seen enough of both genres that I can make that call. I saw Bob Seger and the Silver Bullet Band 7 times. I saw The Rolling Stones 9 times and Bruce Springsteen a half dozen times. Bruce and Bob Seger both sing from their heart. They're not trained singers, but they can touch your emotions.

I talked all the Oaks into going with me to a Springsteen concert and Joe Bonsall really loved him after that. He put on one of the greatest shows I've ever seen. During the show, as I watched Joe's smiling face, I said to him, "I told ya, Joey. I knew you were gonna love this band." We might not have agreed with his stand on many social issues, but we loved him as a performer and musician.

I also love Rod Stewart. His voice is so great, and he has so much feeling and heart and soul. And when "Elvira" and "Bobbie Sue" were huge, I went to see Michael Jackson and the Jacksons at the Nashville Municipal Auditorium. I was honored to get to go backstage to meet Michael. Michael also put on a totally entertaining and very long show.

But many venues limit the time we can be on stage. The casinos in Las Vegas would have a fit if we kept fans away from the slot machines for three hours. We've played Vegas more than just about any place, beginning back during our gospel days. I love Las Vegas, but you probably won't find me sitting at a blackjack table. I was never tempted to gamble. But I enjoy the luxury living, fine food and dining of Vegas, and they have the most incredible entertainment in the world.

In the 1960s and '70s, we'd play cards on the bus. Again, we didn't gamble, and we played just to pass the time. This was long before the internet and cell phones. Back then, we would listen to cassettes and 8-tracks! When video tapes were invented, we got one of the first VCRs so we could watch movies on the road. One movie we watched all the time was "The Last Waltz." Then we transitioned to DVDs, and we rejoiced when satellite TV improved to the point that we could watch it on the bus.

You need to have something to do if you're going to be traveling as much as we have. We averaged over 100, 000 miles a year for 55 years, and that doesn't include the air miles by plane. I have no idea how many buses we have gone through over the years, but I'm sure it is more than 20.

One of the most impressive things about Duane, Joe, Richard and I, and our entire organization has always been our work ethic. For decade after decade, the Oak Ridge Boys never did less than 100 concerts a year, and most years, we did 150 to 250. On days when we weren't on the road, you could probably find us taping a TV show, playing the Grand Ole Opry, or in the recording studio. We had a motto that we used if we had an open day and our agent wanted to book us for something. We'd say, "You call, and we'll come."

Ninety-nine percent of the groups who have managed to have some success have not had the longevity that the Oak Ridge Boys have enjoyed. One reason for that is because it is very hard to find the discipline and commitment from band members and singers who will just plow through anything and everything…every single day, year after year, for decade after decade.

Such a heavy travel schedule, with weeks away from home is a big sacrifice. Those in your family, left back at home are making just as big of a sacrifice as those who are out on the road. But anytime I would start to get down or homesick while out on a long tour, I would remind myself that those in the military service, keeping our freedom, are away from home for a much longer period. They, and their families at home, all give a much bigger sacrifice, even in times of peace.

All those miles on the road might have delayed one of our greatest honors. On July 8, 2011, we were playing the Grand Ole Opry, when country legend Little Jimmy Dickens walked out on stage. He was wearing a long, white beard and sunglasses and looked like a miniature version of me. He told the audience, "All my life, I have wanted to be a little bitty Oak Ridge Boy." We all thought he was just joking around, but he was there for something very important. He invited us to become official members of the Opry.

We had no inkling that we were going to be asked to be members. We were completely blindsided. Jimmy explained that we would become official Opry members the following month. When Little Jimmy asked us to join the Opry, my thoughts immediately went back to when I was little boy, back on the farm in south Alabama, listening to Little Jimmy Dickens on the very same Grand Ole Opry. It was a surreal moment.

On the night of August 6th, we were surprised on the Opry stage once again, when a video message by President George Bush started playing behind us. President Bush said, "I cannot think of any group or person who deserves this honor more." Like he did a month earlier, Little Jimmy Dickens came out to officially welcome us to the Opry family. Standing with him that night was one of the highlights of my life and my career.

We often get asked, "Why did it take the Opry so long to make you members?" We had performed as guests on the Opry for many years. But one reason we hadn't been asked to become members was they used to have a rule that required members to be there for a certain number of Friday and Saturday nights. To be honest, when we were criss-crossing the country and the world, playing to huge arenas, we couldn't afford to give up the highest paying nights of the week, so we could be on the Opry. But when the Opry expanded with shows on Tuesday and Thursday nights, it made it easier for us to give the Opry the time and attention that it deserves from any member.

In 1997, I was honored to become a member of the Alabama Music Hall of Fame. I was so touched that my home state would give me such a wonderful tribute. Lionel Richie, Rose

Maddox and The Speer Family were others who were inducted during the same ceremony.

Three years later, the Oak Ridge Boys were inducted into the Gospel Music Hall of Fame. That event was extra special because we were also joined by every living former member of the group. Those included Jim Hammill, Noel Fox, Ron Page, Gary McSpadden, Willie Wynn, Calvin Newton and Tommy Fairchild. I also met Lon Deacon Freeman for the very first time. He had been one of the original guys in the group. Over the past 20 years, many of those men have passed away, so that night will always be very special to me.

When you're on the road as much as we are, one thing you have to get used to is missing important family events. I regret that I missed so many life moments with my kids. You can also feel helpless when your loved ones back home are sick or even worse, dying. I was in Nashville, Indiana when I got word that my mother was near death. She had been in hospice and wanted to see me before she passed. I did the concert that night and I flew to Brewton. Thankfully, I made it there in time, and was with her when she died.

All of us have lost parents and other family members while we were on tour. But we've lived by the old motto, "The Show Must Go On." As soon as the show was over, we would fly home to be with our loved ones, and as soon as we could, we'd meet back up with the group and walk out on stage like nothing had happened. It is not easy to deal with all the emotions you are going through at that moment.

Some days you are dealing with situations back at home. Your wife might call and say the hot water heater has flooded the house or a tree has fallen on the roof. You feel bad because you can't be there in person. But you can't let those problems weigh you down, when you go on stage. You try to put it in the back of your mind as you do the show. At those moments, you kind of do the concert subconsciously, and everything comes naturally.

Occasionally, when you're "on autopilot," you will forget the words to a song you've sung for 40 years. Something might distract you for a moment and you just go blank. It's a helpless feeling when you forget the words to a song, and the harder you try to come up with the words, the worse it gets, and the band just keeps on playing, hoping you will finally jump in. It usually happens on the older stuff, the songs I've sang forever. The other guys try to cover for you if it happens, but when it's your turn to take the lead, it's tough.

I've forgotten a verse to "Thank God for Kids," and Joe or Duane will try to whisper me a line. They can usually save the day, but it occasionally turns into a giant train wreck. I think the audience actually enjoys seeing that we are all human, and they get a big laugh out of it. But I never wanted to be a comedian, so I'm not looking for laughs when I walk on stage!

In 2000, the year nick-named Y2K, we slowed down enough to visit the town where our group got its name...Oak Ridge, Tennessee. In the early 1940s, as World War II was winding down, thousands of workers, scientists and engineers came to Oak Ridge, just west of Knoxville to work on a top-secret mission for the U.S. government. That mission became known as The Manhattan Project, and the result was development of the atomic bomb.

The early founders of our group, who had been going by the very unglamorous name of "The Georgia Clodhoppers" since 1945, entertained the people of Oak Ridge, Tennessee. They say that the Clodhoppers were the only outside group that was ever allowed inside the Oak Ridge government compound. And the Georgia Clodhoppers put on so many shows there, that they decided to rename their group The Oak Ridge Quartet.

Almost 60 years later, we stopped in Oak Ridge, where they allowed us to tour the atomic energy plant. They took us into a room that had a huge magnetic machine. They warned us it was so powerful it would try to pull the keys out of our pockets. I found it was attracted to the stent I had in my heart, and I could feel it pulling at my chest.

Earlier, I talked about my love of all kinds of music. In 1987, I was able to record a duet with the "Godmother of Soul" Patti Labelle. We did a song called "Rainbow at Midnight" and it appeared on the Oaks' "Where the Fast Lane Ends" album.

Patti and I recorded the song in a studio in Philadelphia. My friend Joe Walsh, of The Eagles, played slide guitar on the song. Patti Labelle has an incredible voice, and when she sang, I called it a "vocal waterfall." A voice like hers is a God gift. Our song turned out great and I loved it. I enjoyed trying new things, and I was at a point in my life where I wanted to branch out a little, stretch my wings and see what I was truly capable of.

SLOW TO LEARN

As I was writing this book, I started trying to think of a good title. I knew it needed to be something catchy, that described me. One of the first possibilities to pop into my mind was "Slow to Learn." We ultimately chose another title for the book, but that phrase did earn the title of this chapter. And yes, it does describe me…unfortunately.

After my divorce, I lived with my girlfriend for 5 or 6 years, before we parted ways. At that time in my life, I really don't think I was cut out to be a married man. To prove that…I got married.

I met a former Las Vegas model.

Her name was Luetta. Her parents owned a big air conditioning and sheet metal company in Las Vegas, and they did work on all the hotels and casinos in Las Vegas. Luetta came to one of our concerts in Lake Tahoe, and we met after the show, and a short time later, we started dating.

Luetta's family was taking some clients to Rome for a vacation, and she invited me to come along. During our time there, the two of us took a train from Rome to Monte Carlo. We had a whirlwind, romantic weekend, and we stayed at a wonderful hotel. And after drinking way too much champagne, I asked her to marry me. I was honestly kind of surprised when she said yes. So surprised that when she asked me to set the date, I said, "How about a year from now?"

At the time, a year seemed like a long way away. But that year sure seemed to pass quickly. On November 10, 1984, my best man Jeff Panzer sat in the back of the limo with me, as we headed toward the wedding. Jeff looked at me and said, "Golden, it ain't too late to back out. We can just drive to the airport and get the hell out of town. Let's go to Mexico." I thought about it for a few seconds and answered, "No, I've let my mouth get me in trouble. Now I've got to keep my word."

We were married fewer than three years.

I guess I could end this chapter there. But that wouldn't be the whole story. If I'm going to write about all the good things I've done in my life, I should be honest enough to also write about the bad.

Luetta and I had a volatile relationship, and it was something I was not used to at all. I had never been around loud households. Growing up, I never heard arguments or cursing in the house. Even after I was grown, I never heard my parents raise their voices with each other. Their vows to "love, honor and cherish" lasted all the way to the grave.

I was not raised around conflicts in the home. I didn't hear a curse word until I was playing football in high school, and our coach gave me a crash course in cussing. So, when the loud and bad words started to fly during my second marriage, I just made myself scarce. I didn't spend much time at home.

I take the blame for my sins. I'm too old to deny what I've done. I need to be honest to my fans, my friends, my family and most of all, to myself. I was never faithful to Luetta. Through a long period of my life, beautiful women were my greatest weakness. I could be strong through a lot of other temptations, but sweet, beautiful women were my downfall. I used to say, "If you're trying to set a trap, if you bait it with a beautiful woman, you will probably catch me."

128

While we were married, I started seeing a couple other women. The craziest and worst incident came when the Oaks were playing in Tahoe. Luetta came to be with me and so did two other women I was seeing. I felt like I was walking a tightrope, and I knew I was going to fall. And I fell hard.

It turned into a huge mess. I somehow survived the fall, but my marriage didn't. If "Trying to love two women, is like a ball and chain," trying to love 3 women was totally impossible. I sang "Trying to Love Two Women" every night, and you would think I would listen to the words.

With each new relationship, I kept thinking, "This time I will act differently." But it always worked out the same way every time. If you try to love more than one woman, if you go out on your wife, you are going to get caught. It only leads to heartache for all concerned. Instead of a bed of roses, you wind up in a patch of thorns.

I wasn't trying to hurt anyone, but I certainly did hurt a lot of people. But that was many years ago. In the latter part of my life, I have been a good husband and I am a good husband today. Yes, I was slow to learn. But better late than never.

GOLDEN ERA

On July 18, 1980, my dad's birthday, I signed a contract that changed my life. It wasn't any kind of musical agreement. It was the contract to my new home. I called the home and all the property I purchased around it, "Golden Era."

When I bought the 15-room plantation home more than 40 years ago, it was out in the country, on a small gravel road between Hendersonville and Gallatin, Tennessee. There were no other homes within a mile. But since then, both towns have built up so much, that there are now hundreds of houses all around me.

My home is an historic place. It was originally called "Pilot's Knob," and it was built by Revolutionary War Colonol James Franklin in 1786. It is the oldest private home in the state of Tennessee and is also the oldest brick home in the state.

In the late '70s, just before I bought the home, they found a bunch of gold hidden inside one of the walls. They said it was buried during the Civil War when Union forces were coming through. I wish that gold would have stayed hidden until I moved in!

But the property's history goes back much farther than the Civil War. Thousands of years ago, at least three different prehistoric Indian tribes occupied the area. I've found hundreds of arrowheads and other ancient artifacts all around our house.

There is a comfort feeling about "Golden Era." It has a slow, lazy feeling as I listen to the Station Camp Creek that's at the edge of our yard. I have spent thousands of hours enjoying that creek. When I'm out on tour, when we get to a new town, I like to go out walking and I always pick up acorns I find on my walks. I bring those home and plant them on my property and after all these years, I now have big oak trees that have come from all around the country.

For a long time, I had a couple teepees set up on the grounds. They're gone now, but my beautiful American flag still waves proudly over my lawn. "Golden Era" has become a sanctuary for wild deer, turkey, squirrels, and lots of birds. I put out feed for the animals each day. I probably spend more on animal feed than I do on food for me and my wife. When I'm home, I like to get up before daylight. I scatter birdfeed out and sit on my patio with a cup of coffee and I watch all the blue jays and red birds come in for breakfast. With all the land around us now covered with houses, our property is one of the few safe places for those animals.

"Golden Era" has also been a home for wayward souls. A lot of people have used it as a safe haven during divorces and other life events. All my sons have lived there at one time. Craig still lives in the cabin on the grounds. When Chris and Rusty were teenagers, they loved living there. When I was on the road, for security at home, I used to hire an off-duty deputy sheriff to park his car in the drive every night. But then I asked Chris and Rusty to move in.

They set up all their band equipment and big speakers in the basement and they could play and rehearse their music as loud as they wanted. And they liked it loud. With our thick, brick basement walls, and with us being so far away from any other houses, my sons could blast their music and have their friends over for parties and we didn't disturb any neighbors.

While it still feels like we are out in the country, we are only a half hour from downtown Nashville. But "Golden Era" really is a place of refuge. The home and grounds have plenty of room to have lots of friends over. Over the last 40 years, a lot of people have visited my home. People from Leon Russell to Booker T. Jones and Tanya Tucker to U.S. senators and governors have been guests here.

Willie Nelson stayed at my house, and we had a great time. Willie was always so nice and genuine, just a great guy. He came to visit me in the early '80's. I don't know why, but people like to ask, "Did you guys smoke any marijuana there?" My answer is, "What do you think?" I love Willie. I was never around him when he was in a bad mood. I can have good days and bad days, and when I am having a bad day, I can be an ass. But Willie was always happy, every single time I was with him.

I played a number of Willie's "Farm Aid" events, and they were so exciting and the crowds were huge. At one of those, I met Joe Walsh, from the Eagles. We became friends and Joe came to visit me in Hendersonville. He stayed with me for 6 or 7 days. He was a character, and this was back in my wild party, bachelor days, so we had a fun-filled week.

Lots of "stars" have visited my home, but to me, everybody that comes here is special. I love to welcome friends and family to my home.

I mentioned all the animals I have on my property, but at one time, I also had camels…whether I wanted them or not. Conway Twitty owned the land right behind my house and his concession manager, Velton Lang, put 3 camels on the property. One day those camels came over and ate a whole row of my pine trees. They even ate a magnolia tree that I had brought from my childhood home in Brewton.

If you've ever driven by my home, you've no doubt noticed the large tree at the entrance gate. In the '80s, for one of my birthdays, my wife Brenda gave me a very special and unique gift. She asked wood carver Roger Webb to turn our tree into a work of art. Roger lived in Gatlinburg and created what he called "spirit faces" in wood.

He carved a huge face in our tree and called it "Father Time." But it looks just like me! A lot of people think it is me, but it's really a spirit face. Over time, the original tree carving started deteriorating, so Roger came back and replaced it with the side of a big cedar tree, and he carved a new face in it.

A lot of fans and tourists stop and take their picture by the tree. It's probably one of the most photographed trees in the state. In recent years, the tree has been hit by numerous storms that have taken the top half away. Right now, the carving is needing a little touch up. It is getting a little aged and pretty weathered…kind of like the guy it looks like!

I don't like to say that I "own" my home. I'm just the caretaker here. It was here a long time before I came along and it will be here long after I'm gone. But I've tried to be a good caretaker for it over the last 4 decades.

YOU'RE FIRED

I'm willing to open up and share some things that are not real pretty, but I ask that you don't think bad of my Oak Ridge Boys partners or of me, at least until you read "the rest of the story."

The Oak Ridge Boys' success continued growing through the 1980s. Our audiences kept expanding, getting bigger and bigger, and as we played the biggest coliseums across the country, we never sang to an empty seat. Every song we released to radio raced up the charts and didn't stop until it hit the very top.

As our list of hit songs grew, so did the length of my beard and hair. I had stopped cutting my beard at the start of the decade and by now, my appearance had drastically changed. I was also going through changes in my personal life.

I became friends with some people who were into the Mountain Man lifestyle. That way of life also attracted me, and it reminded me of my youth, growing up in the woods of southern Alabama. I started learning everything I could about the frontiersman and Native American way of living. As I started really getting into that culture, I found it was a pleasant change of pace after traveling from one city to another. Walking out in the woods was much more calming than running from a hotel room to a big concert arena. So, anytime I had a day off from the road, I would head to the woods to get away from everything. Today, they would call that, "going off the grid."

I also have a passion, love and respect for the Native American people and for their culture. I find it fascinating and interesting, and I started adopting many of their traditions into my own lifestyle. I loved the primitive camping part of it, and I like to build a fire on the ground like the early Indians did. I'd choose a campfire over a blaring TV any day. One of the highest honors I have received was when the Cherokee Indian Association gave me their Entertainer of the Year award.

Over the years, I've been invited to many Indian ceremonies. I attended cleansing and purification ceremonies that medicine men conducted in sweat lodges. They would say beautiful prayers and I always gained a sense of peace that I couldn't find anywhere else. I learned how to burn sage and use the smoke to kill germs and bacteria in the air. I've enjoyed getting to know different Indian tribes, and I've met many local shaman at different places we've performed.

I started wearing buckskins and moccasins, and at one time, I had 3 large teepees. There were rumors that I lived in a teepee. I camped in them, but I never lived in one. I enjoyed putting a fire in my teepee and sitting there in the evenings. It was calming.

Today, my Mountain Man appearance and lifestyle are kind of my trademark. But 35 years ago, my Oak Ridge Boys partners couldn't quite figure it out. They didn't understand why I wanted long hair and an even longer beard. They were also confused on why I would wear animal skin coats and hats. Our fans were also torn. Some loved my new look, while other fans totally hated it.

In 1982, I received a letter from my partners. They made it very clear that they didn't think "the new William Lee" was good for the group. They said my long hair and beard were not good for the group's image. The letter also stated their dislike of my long fingernails and even the way I walked on stage, "Much too slow!" They were also upset because I wore "a dead animal" (a coyote skin) on "The Tonight Show." I thought the letter was very petty, but I was glad to know how they felt. But I knew where my heart was, and I knew I never had ill intentions against anyone. I just ignored the letter. I didn't respond at all.

In April of 1983, People magazine came to my home and took photos of me by my teepee. They wanted to do a feature article on me and asked if I was willing to answer a few questions. I said, "Of course, I will answer anything you ask." I have always been that way. If someone asked a question, no matter how personal it was, or if they asked my opinion, I gave it to them. One of my pet peeves is lying. I just refuse to tell a lie. Of course, telling the truth, the whole truth and nothing but the truth can also get you in trouble…as I was about to find out.

The People magazine reporter asked all his questions, and I answered every one. I was totally honest. When the magazine hit newsstands, it told how the Oak Ridge Boys were no longer in harmony because "Golden has changed his tune." In the article, I admitted to smoking marijuana and snorting a little coke. The story called my lifestyle "decadent." The article also noted an "undeclared cold war" between Duane and me, and it detailed how the two of us had not talked to each other in over a year. And man, the sh!t hit the fan. The other Oaks and our management didn't appreciate the bad publicity.

Before I go any further, I need to say that I am a different man today than I was in the 1980s. During my wild, party years, I never tried to hide my crazy and sometimes dangerous ways. But my party days ended a few decades ago. When my son Solomon came along, I found that being a father was better than any drug I had ever done.

The People magazine article got a lot of attention, but it didn't seem to hurt our career. All our concerts continued to sell out and almost every record we released hit number one. But it seemed the more successful we got, the more of a challenge it was to keep our focus on the music. As our personal differences started to cut deeper, I stopped communicating with the other guys. And they stopped communicating with me.

A little communication could have eased a lot of worries when I recorded a solo album in 1986. When MCA Records released my "American Vagabond" album, my "Thank You's" on the back cover, included one to my producer, Jimmy Bowen. I wrote, "Jimmy, thank you for giving me enough rope to ??" Yes, I might have been given just enough rope to hang myself. And Richard, Joe and Duane sure wanted to string me up. They didn't understand why I wanted to do a project outside of the group. They also might have started thinking I wanted to leave the group or I wanted to be a "star" on my own. Neither of those was correct. But since we weren't talking, none of them asked me, and I didn't bother trying to tell them.

At the time, we had three buses. The singers had one, the band was on one and the crew rode the third bus. Throughout the entire year, I was on the same bus with the other guys and I didn't talk to anyone. Yes, I can be quiet. Don't ever try to get into a "let's be quiet" contest with me. I will win every time.

But there were no winners during that stressful and sad time. Looking back, if there was just one thing we could have, and should have done differently, it is this...we should have continued talking to each other. But instead, we got even quieter. I know I did.

None of the Oaks ever got into a loud argument. We never had shouting matches and wouldn't have dreamed of getting into a physical altercation. But sometimes silence can do just as much damage. During an 8-hour bus ride, in total silence, your mind and imagination can start to run, and you start to wonder what the other guys are thinking about.

But things finally came to a head in March of 1987. I found out that I was being fired by the Oaks in a pretty crazy way. I heard about it from a fan.

We had played a concert in Detroit and were looking forward to a few months off. When I saw that Bob Seger was playing at the Joe Louis Arena the night after our show, I decided to stay an extra night in Detroit.

I was walking through the hotel lobby, when a fan who traveled everywhere to see us, came up to me and she was crying. She asked, "What happened? Why are they firing you?" I couldn't believe my ears. A fan had heard the news before I did.

I felt the other guys had been acting strange and even more distant, but I never expected this. I went to the Bob Seger concert, but I had a hard time enjoying or even concentrating on the show. My mind was racing as I thought back over the last 20 years. It's not a good feeling when you see your career and your paycheck coming to a sudden end.

The next day, Brenda (who would later become my wife) at the Oaks' office, called me and said there was a letter for me from the other three guys, telling me that I was out of the group. I was devestated. I felt betrayed by my partners. Our manager Jim Halsey called it one of the saddest days of his life. Mine too.

I was never consulted about the decision for me to leave the group. It was their choosing and I had no choice in it. It was all their decision. We never had a meeting about anything, and I felt like I at least deserved to have a meeting before I was let go. My sadness soon turned to anger as I thought back to the role I played in getting each of my partners their jobs with the group.

When I came back home to Hendersonville, my phone was ringing off the wall. I didn't even try to play back all the messages that had completely filled up my machine. One of the first calls I took was from my ex-wife Frogene. She was as mad as a setting hen, saying, "William, I am so angry. You did not deserve this." She explained that Gordon Stoker of The Jordanaires had called her and he was very upset. She told me Gordon kept saying, "This is not right."

I was going through every emotion there was, when my son Chris called. He and Rusty were recording songs for their new album, and they asked me to come to the studio to sit in on their session. Chris said, "Dad, you need to get away from that phone and come hang out with us." They recorded "Blonde Ambition" and "Country Comfort" that day, and I sang background on both of those. It was good for me to "get right back on the bike" after the hard, nasty fall I had just taken.

I was still trying to process everything, when my best friend Jeff Panzer called to tell me his father had died. Jeff asked if he could share a memory from that time here:

> "Just after William was fired, my father passed away. The last person I expected to see knocking on my sister's door in Long Island, New York was William Lee Golden. This man had just lost his career, and he didn't know what the hell he was going to do. But he put all that aside for a friend.
>
> William slept on my sister's basement floor because he didn't want to go to a hotel. He wanted to be there with all my family. That was a life lesson that he taught me, that I never forgot. A couple years later, when his father Luke passed away, I just knew that I had to get down to Brewton, Alabama. I was in the middle of a couple of shoots, but I flew down to be with William. Your true friends are a select few. And when those friends need you, you've got to be there."   – Jeff Panzer

Immediately after my firing, every TV and radio show and every newspaper and magazine wanted to get my side. I turned down every request. Barbara Walters with the "20/20" TV show wanted me for an exclusive interview, and again, I declined. But when I got word that the Oaks were going to introduce my replacement, I knew that I needed to finally address what happened.

Just hours before the Oak's press conference to announce Steve Sanders as their new member, they were met by a Nashville newspaper headline that informed them, (and the world) that I was filing a lawsuit against them. When I saw their faces at the press conference, I could tell they were in shock.

During my time away from the Oak Ridge Boys, I found out who my real friends were. I also found out who were my fair-weather friends. I figured that would save me a lot of time and trouble the next time around, because I would already know who my true friends were.

One of my true friends was Johnny Cash. In my lowest moments, Johnny called and invited me to come over to his home. We'd get in his jeep and he'd drive me all around his property. He let me hang out and I visited his home quite a few times. John was a friend in good times and in bad.

I walked around in a daze for about a half year after the Oaks voted me out. But I finally pulled myself together. Someone told me that everyone gets knocked down, but the winners are those who can get back up. It was time for me to get up and get on with my life.

The same year I was fired by the Oaks, I also found myself single again. My second wife and I divorced. A short time later, I lost my recording contract with MCA Records. A year later, my father died. It was a bad time, probably the lowest of my life.

I returned to Brewton to spend some time with my mother in our old homeplace. While I was in Alabama, I tried to reassess who I was, where I was in my career, and why I was there. I never forgot where I came from, and I knew I could also get a better understanding of my future when I was down on the farm.

I started clearing out some fence rows as I tried to clear my mind. I put a new fence around my childhood home, and I planted some trees in honor of my dad. When I came back to Hendersonville, I brought some trees with me and they are still standing in my yard today.

As I put each tree in the ground, I also buried every grudge I had with anyone I felt had done me wrong. I covered them with dirt forever, and I hoped anyone I had ever done wrong might do the same for me. And like those trees I planted, I was ready to rise above everything that was now in the past.

When I left the Oaks, they also fired some of the band members too, including Don Breland, Skip Mitchell and a couple guys who were tour managers, Raymond Hicks and Charlie Daunis. It was a sweeping change that got rid of the guys who were close to me.

But that group of talented men would continue to stay close as they joined up with my sons. Chris and Rusty were just starting to get some attention as a country duo, going by The Goldens. The entire group used my house as their practice and rehearsal space. Since I was home, trying to get my own act together, I would walk down to the basement and start singing with them. We had such a great time, and made such good music, that we decided that I would join them on the road.

I also returned to the studio to record some new music. My long-time friend Tony Brown cut a couple songs with me. One was called "Louisiana Red Dirt Highway," and when Harold Shedd, the head of Mercury Records heard it, he offered me a recording contract. Tony, Harold and Buddy Cannon helped me make some great music at Mercury. The first single released to radio was a positive song called "Keep Looking Up." I could relate to its lyrics, "When life knocks you down, get back up for another round."

My second solo single was the song that had landed me the record contract, "Louisiana Red Dirt Highway." We filmed a music video for that song at the farm where I grew up in Alabama. I wore my high school FFA jacket in the video. My mother also appeared in the video, as she stood by her mailbox, waving at me. My solo efforts didn't get a lot of radio airplay, but the music videos were very popular. "Louisiana Red Dirt Highway" was the number one music video for three weeks in a row.

Jim Halsey continued to manage me after I left the Oaks, and he was able to get me quite a few television spots. One of the most memorable was the night I was a guest on Ralph Emery's "Nashville Now" show on The Nashville Network. After my first song, I went over to be interviewed by Ralph, and I was met by Ralph and Porter Wagner, who were both wearing long beards that they had glued on. They both wore the beards for my entire interview.

One night, my friend Johnny Cash invited me to a party at his house. He told me that a lot of country music stars would be there. When I arrived, I saw many old friends I hadn't seen in a few years. Those included all the Oak Ridge Boys. That was the first time I had been in a social setting with all the guys since our breakup. None of us had any major conversation that night, but it was good to see Richard, Joe and Duane again.

THE GOLDENS

Have you ever been fired from a job? If it was a job you had been at for many years, or one you really loved, it can be devastating. At first, you might think you can't even survive it. But as time goes on, you go through a variety of feelings. At first, you are hurt, then you get angry, and finally you pull yourself together and get on with your life.

I went through all of that when I was let go by the Oaks. But God works in mysterious ways. What I thought was the end of the world, actually turned out to be a wonderful blessing in disguise. While I was out of the group, I was given the chance to enjoy 9 awesome years with my sons Chris, Rusty and Craig.

With Rusty being the older brother, he had mastered both the drums and piano, by the time Chris got into music. But Chris was very competitive and whatever Rusty would play, Chris would watch him and then he'd try to play the same thing. He did that with the drums and piano.

Epic Records released an album on Chris and Rusty simply called "The Goldens" in 1987. They were getting ready to go on tour, and since I now had some time on my hands, they decided to add one more Golden to their lineup. I wanted to continue entertaining, and I wasn't about to turn my back on singing, just because I was out of the Oaks. Skip Mitchell and Don Breland, from the Oaks Band, both signed on. Skip had been with the Oaks since 1976, and Don had been with the group since '71.

Greg Gordon, who had played for the Oaks off and on from 1965 to '71 also joined The Goldens.

Jimbeau Hinson also joined us on a lot of shows. Jimbeau wrote the Oaks' huge number one "Fancy Free" with Roy August. There was never a dull moment when Jimbeau was around.

To play drums for The Goldens, I brought in Buster Phillips. Buster was a session drummer and he played on a lot of hit songs. But Buster had started drinking, and alcohol really took over his life. He moved to South Carolina and when he heard I was out of the Oaks, he called me to tell me how sorry he was. He confided how his career and life had been ruined by alcohol. I told him he had too much talent to go out that way. I also told him, "We're getting ready to go out on the road and make some music. If you can hitch hike to Nashville, you can stay with me, and you can be our drummer."

Then I made sure he knew what was expected of him. "But you can't stay here and get drunk every day. I'm gonna get you out and we're going to walk every day. I will get you in shape, and you're not going to sit around, drinking all the time." I am happy to say that I helped get Buster off the alcohol. He got that fire back in his eyes. We walked 6 miles a day, and some days, I would walk double that. Buster did a wonderful job for us and we made some great music together. I love Buster.

As we toured the country, I was able to spend time with my sons and get to know them as young men, and they got to know me as a man and as a father. While Chris and Rusty were in the spotlight, my son Craig was also a part of The Goldens, as he worked as their road manager and bus driver. Craig also set up the stage, ran lights and sound and sold T-shirts, CDs and photos. Here are some of my son's memories of those years:

> "Those years were truly The Golden years. I loved it and we had the best time.

I drove for my brothers and my dad, and that led to me becoming a full-time driver for other artists. It's ironic that my mom drove a bus and now I do. She drove a school bus, which she owned herself. She loved it when I got into driving buses.

As The Goldens, we played every honky-tonk in the country. When dad was with the Oaks, they were selling out huge arenas and now he was playing little clubs. It would be a tough change for anybody, but he handled it very well. The crowds were smaller, but dad wanted to make sure that he thanked each and every person who came to see us. At every concert we ever did, he stayed until he had signed autographs for every single person who wanted one. I would have to go get him and almost drag him to the bus. He would take time with everybody, and he still does that today."

— Craig Golden

"When the Oaks let dad go, it was a big blow. But it turned out to be such a blessing for all of us. I was able to get to know my dad in a way I never had. We were able sing and play with him for almost a decade. I spent more time with him during that time than I ever did in my whole life. When we were touring, we were together 24/7. I would never have gotten to do that with my father had he stayed with the Oak Ridge Boys.

The Goldens and Dad played everything from stadiums to little clubs and honky-tonks. We rehearsed our show at the Bell Cove Club in Hendersonville, and then we started having actual shows there. It was there that we started putting on marathon concerts. Dad had seen a few Bruce Springsteen shows and Bruce would sing 4 or 5 hours. We started doing the same thing. Dad would come out and tell the crowd, "I feel like singin' all night!" and he would.

Almost as soon as we started touring as The Goldens, Charlie Daniels asked us to perform at his "Volunteer Jam." We were so excited, and we told everyone we knew that we were going to be on the Jam. But four days before the show, they called to say they didn't have room for us. We were so bummed.

But the night before the event, they called again and said they wanted us to be the first act on the show. The Jam ran from noon to midnight, with all the big stars not going on stage until that night. Since we were supposed to go on at noon, we knew they were basically using us as their soundcheck. The crowd would still be coming in and those who were there, wouldn't be paying that much attention.

We were ready to go on at noon, but for some reason, they kept putting us off. They brought on other acts and kept telling us that we would be next. We stood there waiting... for over 8 hours! That night, the group Lynyrd Skynyrd reunited for the very first time in over a decade. 17, 000 people were holding lighters as Skynyrd sang their final song. At that moment, the stage manager yelled to us, 'OK boys, you're on next!' We had thought we were going to be the show's sound check, and instead, we had to follow Lynyrd Skynyrd.

One of our most memorable shows was only the second one we did. We played 'Farm Aid' at Memorial Stadium in Lincoln, Nebraska. It was epic, with 72, 000 people in attendance. As we left on the bus after the show, Pete Cummings, who played guitar for us, said, 'Well boys, that's it for me. I'm done. It's not going to get any bigger than that.'

We performed at four Farm Aids, two in Texas, one in Indianapolis and one in Lincoln, Nebraska. The Indianapolis Farm Aid was another incredible event, because my hero Elton John made a surprise appearance. Guns and Roses, Don Henley and Bruce Hornsby were also on the show. During dad's set, Willie Nelson, Kris Kristofferson and Joe Walsh joined him on a couple songs.

The Goldens and dad had different booking agents, but they all worked together, and they would offer us all together as a big show. We opened concerts for a lot of big acts, and we headlined a lot of shows on our own. We had a great live show and we always got invited back to every place that booked us."

— Rusty Golden

"My dad was always a little bit ahead of his time. He was a visionary, who set a lot of trends in music and fashion. He broke the rules and made some new ones.

Dad has a building on his property that's an Indian ceremonial chamber, and we put in a studio and cut some songs there. Dad and The Goldens did a lot of TV stuff, especially on The Nashville Network. Rusty and I were getting some radio and music video airplay, and as a solo artist, dad had a number one video with "Louisiana Red Dirt Highway."

I can tell you from first-hand experience, that The Goldens had more fun on the road than the Oaks did. I was in both groups, and when the Oak Ridge Boys did a west coast tour every year, we drove straight there and straight back. We never had time to stop and see the country. But when dad and the Goldens headed west, we were on the road and I said, "We're not far from the

Grand Canyon." Dad said, "I've never seen it." I couldn't believe it. The Oaks had gone by the Grand Canyon dozens of times, but they never had time to go see it.

One of my favorite stories about dad took place out west. I was with a group called Cedar Creek, and we were playing The Palomino Club in Hollywood. Dad came to watch us, and Jerry Lee Lewis was also in the audience. Jerry Lee had one of those big booths that looks like a horseshoe. Dad pulled up a chair and sat next to Jerry Lee, and during the show, our lead singer introduced dad and took the mic out to him. They put the spotlight on dad and when he stood up to wave to the crowd, his chair knocked everything off the table. The drinks just soaked Jerry Lee. Dad took the mic and said, "I'm sure sorry for baptizing Jerry Lee Lewis in front of everyone." Jerry got up from his wet seat and he sat up on the back of his booth for the rest of the show.

Dad had a similar accident happen at a Barbara Mandrell concert in Las Vegas. It was a dinner show, and dad was sitting right in the front. During dinner, he thought his shirt was untucked, so he tucked it in the front of his pants. With his long beard, he couldn't see that he had actually put the tablecloth into his pants.

In the middle of the show, Barbara introduced dad, and when he stood up to wave to the crowd, he pulled that entire table full of plates and drinks right off into the floor. Everyone was grabbing at the glasses as the big spotlight shined brightly right on him.

One of the best things about my dad is how he is able to see the good and the promise in other people. He brought Wayne Halper to Nashville. Wayne was a trained pianist who played a solo at Carnegie Hall when he was only 12 years old. When he moved to Nashville, he stayed at dad's house for a few weeks. Wayne went on to be the main legal guy at Capitol Records and then became the General Manager of DreamWorks Records.

Dad also saw greatness in Kay Shaw, and when she moved to Nashville to work for RCA Records, dad hired her to work part-time for him. She stayed at his house while she got settled in Music City, and Kay went on to become one of the premiere newspaper, magazine and book writers in Nashville, and then became George Strait's long-time PR person.

In the fall of 1995, we started hearing rumors that the Oaks might be interested in bringing dad back. Rusty and I knew that would be the end of our touring with him, but we understood that it would be a good move for him. We were thankful for the 9 years we had together. Many acts don't last 9 years, so we were happy to cheer our dad on as he entered a new chapter of his life and career."

— Chris Golden

THE PRODIGAL RETURNS

"If I can't be a favorite son, I'll be the prodigal one…'Cause I've been gone too long."

Roger Murrah and Scott Anders wrote the lyrics to "Ozark Mountain Jubilee," but they were words that described me perfectly. It was like Roger and Scott were looking right into my heart.

The last 9 years had not been easy, but as I toured the country with my sons, we had kept the bills paid, while we continued entertaining our fans.

The past 9 years had also not been easy for the Oak Ridge Boys. Their hit records weren't coming like they once had, and their concert bookings were also lagging. But just like The Goldens, the Oaks had continued to entertain their fans.

But the man who took my place, Steve Sanders was going through a rough period.

I won't get into his troubles, but the Nashville press didn't help his problems. The local newspapers ran numerous stories on Steve's marital troubles, which were really no one else's business.

The negative publicity embarrassed the Oak Ridge Boys. I knew if my People magazine article a decade earlier had caused so many problems, that the negative stories about Steve were sure to be even more worrisome.

Steve tried his best to get his personal life in order, but on November 4, 1995, on the afternoon of a show in Fort Worth, Texas, Steve told Duane, Joe and Richard that he was leaving the group…immediately. The guys were scheduled to go on stage that night, now with 3/4 of a group. Duane called his 22-year-old son Dee in Nashville, and asked him to come fill in. Dee caught the next plane to Texas and got there 20 minutes before the Oaks walked out on stage.

Dee sang with the group for the next month. When Dee had to return to college, Duane's son-in-law, Paul Martin, who had been in the group Exile for a couple years, filled in for the rest of December.

During that time, the group called Jim Halsey. Jim had retired as their manager while I had been away. They asked him what they needed to do to become a major act and get back on top again. They also asked him to come back as their manager.

A short time later, they met in person with Jim. At that meeting he told them, "Gentlemen, I have written a 50-point plan that will put the Oaks back where they once were and will get you back into the mainstream of country music." Then he announced, "The first point is…Get back William Lee Golden. You have to get William back in the group. If you don't do that, none of the other 49 points will help."

Jim told the guys that if I returned to the group, that he would also return as the Oaks' manager.

I had a feeling the call was coming. I was playing with The Goldens in Jackpot, Nevada when I got word that they were possibly going to ask me back. I had already heard about the struggles the group was having, and a few years earlier, Richard Sterban had come to see me perform at the Bell Cove Club in Hendersonville. As we visited, he said, "Golden, we made a mistake. We didn't do you right."

As Christmas neared, each of the guys, Joe, Richard and Duane all came individually to talk to me. Joe was the first to pay me a visit. We had run into each other while we were shopping at Kroger's. I kind of felt like a Christmas miracle was happening right there on aisle 5. As soon as I got home, my phone rang and it was Joe. I invited him to come over. A couple days later, Richard paid me a visit. Joe and Richard couldn't have been nicer. Joe said, "Let's throw it all in the sea of forgetfulness, like the Bible says. Let's shake hands and look each other in the eye and say, 'We love each other.' Let's go be the Oak Ridge Boys."

When I met with Duane, he honestly admitted that he was still leery of me rejoining the group. He wasn't sure it would work, and he asked if I would come back on a "90-day trial basis." I said that I would. (At the end of that time, I never did hear anything either way, so maybe I'm still on trial!)

But as Duane and I visited, we both saw how we had grown as performers, but more importantly, grown as men over the past 9 years we were apart. Duane said, "William, in order for us to sing in harmony, we must live in harmony." And from that moment, we have all made a conscious effort to live in harmony with each other.

The decision was made that I would rejoin the group on New Year's Eve. But we would keep my return as an official member a secret, until the moment I stepped out on stage when the Oaks rang in the New Year at the Star Plaza Theatre in Merrillville, Indiana.

My son Chris drove me from Hendersonville to Indiana. Bob Kinkaid, who had been an agent with Jim Halsey, also rode with us. I was Godfather to Bob's daughter, and Bob really pushed for the Oaks to ask me to come back. Since he booked the Oak's dates back when I was in the group and after I left, he got to hear a lot of the comments from concert buyers. Bob was very instrumental in me rejoining the group.

The Oaks did the first part of the concert on their own, as I secretly waited backstage. As I listened to the show, I wondered if I was doing the right thing. The fans had no idea what was about to happen, and neither did I. But any worries I had, came to an end when Joe Bonsall introduced me very simply with, "We would like to go into 1996 as the Oak Ridge Boys…Golden…"

When I walked out on stage, that audience erupted. They cheered for almost 10 minutes. I shook hands with Dee Allen and Paul Martin, who had been filling in over the past two months, and then I received the most sincere and loving hugs I have ever gotten, as Richard, Duane and Joe each welcomed me back.

Bob Kinkaid was at the side of the stage, crying like a baby, and he was not the only one. There were tears of joy throughout that concert hall. Many people just stood there weeping. We started singing 'One in A Million' and that classic Oak Ridge Boys sound was there. Our harmonies came back instantly. It was like we had never missed a day.

I was so excited to be singing with these guys again. It was emotional and exhilarating. When I rejoined the group, I felt the same excitement that I had when I first joined the Oak Ridge Boys in 1965. Yes, it was the most memorable New Year's Eve of my life.

Richard, Duane, Joe and I came together as men and we put all the differences we had in the past. We have true respect for each other man. We regained our focus and vision for the group, and we've not lost that focus over the last two and a half decades.

I wanted to give each of my partners a chance to weigh in with their thoughts on this chapter of our lives:

> "Golden was the guy who would buck every trend and do things his own way. He liked to say, 'I'm gonna dig in

my heels.' Sometimes when he'd dig in his heels, he could be a real pain in the can. But there is nobody who has a bigger heart than William Lee Golden.

Golden is the face of the Oak Ridge Boys to many people. When people think of the Oaks, they think of that guy with the beard. Of course, he's much more than that. Our fans just love him, and I do too."

— Joe Bonsall

"William Lee and I have been very close through our whole career, through all our triumphs and also through our difficult times. Even during the time he wasn't with us, we would still talk. We've been through a lot together, and the good things that we've experienced together are far, far more than any bad.

As William mentioned earlier, we came up with a saying, but it's really how I feel...I love singing in harmony, but it's even better to live in harmony. And living in harmony with William Lee has always been very special to me. Our families are really close. I love all the Golden family.

We have grown closer as we've aged. We've learned to appreciate what each other brings to the stage. I will always be thankful that William was a part of the Oak Ridge Boys, who gave me a job. I'm thankful that God has blessed us through so many years, and I don't see it ending anytime soon."

— Duane Allen

"The Oak Ridge Boys love doing what we do. We realized a long time ago that we need each other, and we decided to pull together as a team. We have a special relationship that exist between the four of us.

> We were so different and that was a secret to the success of the Oak Ridge Boys. Each man in the group was different. Each man brought something different to the table and that was a big part of our appeal. At the same time, over the course of the years, we have learned to respect that difference that exist between the four of us.
>
> We are a true brotherhood. What we do together, singing and making the harmony we do on stage...that same harmony also binds us together off stage. That is one of the reasons for our longevity."
>
> — Richard Sterban

When I rejoined the group, I asked my son Chris to go on tour with us. He played acoustic guitar, mandolin, and harmonica, and I paid him out of my own money. The Oaks eventually hired Chris to be our fulltime drummer, and he was on the road with us for 17 years.

I hate to end this happy chapter on a sad note, but I need to add one last thing.

At one time I had been very close with Steve Sanders. But once he took my place in the group, I never heard from him again. I wish we could have stayed in touch, and I would have welcomed him anytime he called. I would have loved to have tried to help him as he dealt with the struggles he was going through. But that was not to be.

On June 10, 1998, Steve died from a self-inflicted gunshot wound. He was only 45 years old. He was such a great talent and a wonderful guy. He did not deserve to go out the way he did. He left this Earth much too soon.

BRENDA AND SOLOMON

After reading about my earlier marriages, many people might be surprised to know that I have actually been married almost 50 years…total!

Twenty three of those years were with my third wife Brenda. We met when she was working as a receptionist in the Oaks' office. As I got to know her, I was impressed with her appreciation for classical music. She had majored in music and played classical piano. Her talent at classical piano was one of the things that most attracted me to her. I respected the drive and commitment she had as she made the most of her musical gift.

I eventually hired Brenda to be my assistant. She helped me with my fan mail and business dealings, and she also answered my phone, which rang almost around the clock.

By the time we got married, on January 5, 1990, I had been out of the Oaks for 3 years. Brenda stood by me for the 9 years I was away from the group. Those years were difficult financially and emotionally, and Brenda was there for me during those hard times. She was a strong support and an encourager, and I thank her for that.

Without a doubt, the best thing that came out of our marriage was our son. On August 10, 2001, William Solomon Golden was born. Brenda and I had been married 11 and a half years when Solomon finally came into the world. He was a gift from God.

Of course, Brenda was a lot younger than me. I was 62 when our son was born! But he came along at the perfect time. It was a wonderful, joyful experience that I am so thankful for. What a blessed opportunity to experience fatherhood once again.

I also felt that I had done such a bad job of being a father for Craig, Chris and Rusty, that this might be a chance to redeem myself. Rusty, Chris and Craig never complained, and we were all very close as they grew into men. But when they were little, I was gone all the time. The Oaks were on the road over 200 days a year when my first 3 boys were young. When I finally came home, I'd try to give each one of them some of my time, but it was never enough.

I vowed that I would be a different kind of father to Solomon. And I kept that vow. I went on vacations with Brenda and Solomon. We traveled and I took him places that none of my other sons got to go. When he was young, he had all my attention. I didn't have to split my attention between 3 sons like I did with Craig, Chris and Rusty.

When I think back to Solomon's childhood, there are a few moments that will always stand out. One was a silly Halloween night that we spent together. I was going to take Solomon trick-or-treating and we came up with a crazy and impossible idea.

We decided to go to each of the other Oak Ridge Boys' homes to trick-or-treat. I knew Richard, Joe and Duane were all home, and they were going to be passing out candy to the children who knocked on their door. But while we got the treats, we were also going to play a great trick on each of the Oaks.

Brenda dyed my beard dark black and pulled it all up to where it didn't look so long. I put my hair all up, under a Tennessee ball cap. I covered my face with a realistic silicone mask that totally changed my appearance and then I added big glasses and fake, buck teeth. I also wore a Tennessee jersey and orange shorts. Solomon's face was covered, as he dressed as a Storm Trooper.

We went to each Oak's home and while Solomon got the candy, I stood behind him. As Joe, Richard and Duane were getting ready to say goodbye to the Storm Trooper, I silently held out a color 8x10 photo and Sharpie pen. Each of the boys took the photo, signed it, and then handed it back to the buck-toothed, dorky looking Tennessee fan. None of them had a clue who we were!

When we got back home, I posted a picture of me holding the autographed photo to our Facebook page. The other guys couldn't believe the trick we had pulled off. You can decide if you would have recognized me, when you see the picture in the photo section of this book.

Since I sang in hundreds of churches for many, many years, people might be shocked to know that I had never been baptized. They'd be even more shocked to find out that I was 40 years old before I had ever read a complete book of the Bible. I had been raised in the church; I sang in our church when I was just a boy; I had always believed in Jesus Christ, and I had been in one of the greatest gospel groups of all-time, but I had never truly committed myself to the Lord.

My son Solomon had been baptized at the First Baptist Church in Hendersonville. And when he found out I had never been baptized, he told me, "Dad, I want you to be with me in Heaven."

I heard Bishop Joseph Walker preach at Tennessee Titan Steve McNair's funeral. I wanted to meet Bishop Walker, so I visited the Mt. Zion Baptist Church in Nashville. It's a predominately black church and they have great choir music. I really felt the spirit there. After having a sincere, very serious conversation with Bishop Walker, I was finally baptized. It was a very special day.

After all those years of being a gospel singer, it took my little boy to talk me into getting baptized. I think this would be a good place to let Solomon share some of his memories:

"I was very close to God at an early age, and it was very important to me to make sure my dad was saved. It was a great moment for me, and our family when he got baptized.

One of my favorite memories of my dad is something very simple. When I was little, I used to lay back on my dad on the couch, and we would watch the National Geographic channel or Animal Planet on TV. I was very comfortable and happy, and I miss those simpler times.

Music always filled our home. There was always music of all kinds being played. I started playing the violin when I was 2 years old. Dad also bought me drums and a guitar. I'm not very good at either of those, but I am pretty good at violin.

But I have never had any aspirations of being a singer or entertainer. I'm currently going to college, double majoring in Russian and I'm also getting my paramedics degree. I want to be a SWAT medic, and my long-term goal is to work with Homeland Security.

When people find out that William Lee Golden is my father, some of them think, 'You've had everything handed to you, and your life is perfect.' But that is not the way it is. Whether someone is famous or not, we all go through hard times. Things are not always fine and dandy, and bad things happen to everyone. We are all human.

Probably the most annoying thing about being his son is anytime we go out to dinner, there's always someone asking for an autograph. I know that comes with his job, but it took some getting used to for the other family members.

The best thing about having him as my dad has been that he is always there to talk to when I need someone. Since I've been working and in college, it's been harder for me to see dad, but I want to spend more time with him. I know that he is always there for me when I call."

——Solomon Golden

One of the most traumatic days of Solomon's life came when he was just 4 years old. It was April 6, 2006…the day our lives almost ended.

I was enjoying a day off the road, and as I spent some quality time with my family, I didn't pay much attention to the weather forecast. But before the day was over, 48 tornadoes would tear through the southern part of the country.

12 people in Middle Tennessee lost their lives to the tornadoes that day. That number could very easily have been 15, as the worst of those storms rolled directly through our home.

Our home had already been destroyed by one tornado. In 1892, a direct hit from a tornado changed it from a two-story to a one story in just an instant. So, what are the odds that the same home would get hit by a second tornado? Well, it took more than 100 years, but it happened.

Brenda, Solomon and I had been out to lunch, and were headed home when I got a call from Brenda's brother Billy. He yelled, "You guys better get in your basement. A tornado is headed in that direction!" I said, "We're not home yet. We'll be there in a couple minutes." He said, "You'd better hurry." As we watched the sky darken, I drove as fast as I could the rest of the way home.

163

The tornado was on the ground for 14 miles from Goodlettsville to the north side of Gallatin…with us right in the middle. As it tore through, it was picking cars up and tossing them like toys. We turned into our driveway as the tornado came barreling toward us.

We ran straight to our basement. I turned on the TV we had down there, just as the weatherman announced, "The tornado is still on the ground and it is approaching the Station Creek area"…exactly where we were. At that moment, our power went off, and the wind started to whip. We could see out the window and debris and dirt were flying sideways. I told Brenda to get away from the windows and we went into a bathroom under the stairs.

Brenda got on her knees and started praying, and the louder she prayed, the louder the wind got. We could hear what sounded like a continuous roar and then I heard the roof rip off the house. The roar just kept going, and it felt like my eyes were going to pop out. The pressure and suction vacuum from the tornado was so powerful, that I thought my ears were going to explode.

The tornado probably lasted 30 seconds, but it felt like it was never going to end. Finally, the wind stopped, and the only sound was Brenda still praying.

After the tornado passed, I opened the basement door and looked up to the first floor. I could see the sky. There was no second floor. It was all completely gone. I said, "We have been hit bad. The tornado rolled right through our house."

Brenda and Solomon were both crying, as we walked outside and saw all the damage. Both our cars were destroyed, and all our trees were down.

I tried to stay calm as I whispered to my family, "Don't worry about this. Everything here is just stuff and we are all safe."

A man who played steel guitar at the Opry was on his way to pick up his daughter at the school just across the road from us. When the storm hit, he had to stop right in front of our house. He told me he watched as the funnel came down and hit our house and the roof just exploded. Then the funnel raised up and then came back down and hit us again. Then it did the same a third time, until the second floor was totally gone. He thought if any of us were in the house, we were all dead.

It was a close call. The tornado was devastating. But it sure could have been a lot worse. We could easily have all died that day.

I told my wife and son, "There is a reason and a purpose for everything." I had no idea what that purpose was, but I would find out later, as it was the best thing that could have happened to that old house. We ended up taking it back to its original grandeur.

When the residence had been destroyed by the first tornado in 1890, it was just after the Civil War and funds were tight. To save money, they lowered the roof and gave the home a bungalow look. But when we rebuilt it again, we took it back to what it originally looked like when it was first constructed. We elevated the walls about 10 feet, raised the roof, and also made a larger porch.

Cleaning up and rebuilding was a very long process. It took a year to get back into our house. We lived in a motor home in the driveway for 3 months, while we fixed up our little cabin next door. Luckily, our motor home was in the shop being repaired when the tornado hit. I always parked it under a big maple tree and that tree fell right where the motor home would have been. If it hadn't been in the shop, it would have been destroyed. So, even though it was pretty cramped quarters for a few months, my family was thankful to have it.

We lived in the cabin for the last 9 months as we totally rebuilt our home. Thankfully, we had good insurance that paid to replace the home as it was, and with that and another half million dollars of my own money, we made the home much better than it ever was.

My family, including my son Solomon will never forget that day. Today, as I write this, Solomon is 19 years. He is a terrific, smart, handsome, talented, athletic young man. He's strong, and he can beat me at arm wrestling. I'm already very proud of the man he has become, and all of my sons never cease to amaze me.

My four sons are four individual characters. Each one is totally unique, and they are their own individual. They have different likes and dislikes. They are brothers, but they are totally different people. But they are also similar in some very important ways. They all have good hearts. They are all kind, and they all have a love for their mother. Every man should love his mother, and my sons all do.

I tried to find out what each of my sons were interested in, and what they were into. I took them to concerts and to see other people perform. Of course, I tried to take them all to as many of the Oak Ridge Boys shows as I could.

I want to encourage Solomon to be what he wants to be. I want him to do something that will make him happy. I'm so thankful I lived long enough to see him become a young man. Having him at the time in life that I did helped keep me young. It still does.

PRESIDENTS AND HEROES

Back when I was singing in the cotton and peanut fields of Alabama, I could never have imagined that I would go on to sing for, and become friends with, multiple U.S. Presidents.

The Oak Ridge Boys have sung for Presidents Carter, Reagan, Clinton and both President Bushes. But it was the 41st President, George Herbert Walker Bush, who I became the closest with.

President Bush loved country music and he was a huge fan of the Oak Ridge Boys. He had bought all our albums long before we ever met, and he listened to those so much that he knew all the album cuts, not just the songs that were released to radio.

We met George Bush for the first time on October 6, 1983, when he was Vice President under President Ronald Reagan. We were doing an afternoon soundcheck as we prepared to perform at a Congressional barbecue at the White House, and Vice President Bush came literally running across the White House lawn to meet us. He explained that he had to leave town on business, and couldn't stay for the show. He was so disappointed, and he asked if we could sing a couple songs for him right then. Of course, we were glad to.

That night, we performed for President Reagan, his wife Nancy and the other leaders of the nation who were in attendance. You can see a video of that entire concert on

YouTube. It shows Ronald Reagan having the time of his life as he watched us perform. The First Lady was actually dancing in the aisle! After our show, the couple came up on stage and both of them shook hands with every member of our group. I kissed Mrs. Reagan's hand. You could tell that they thoroughly enjoyed our show.

I became close with both President Bush and also his son George W., who became the 43rd U.S. President. They both knew me and accepted me just the way I was. They knew my good points and my bad. I didn't have to "put on airs" when I was with them. I was blessed to get to know both of them in a very personal way. The Bush family were all wonderful Americans. They all grew up loving our country. They loved Democrats and they loved Republicans, and they just loved people.

President Bush and his wife Barbara allowed us into their home and into their world. With my extremely meager and humble background, I was honored when they made me feel welcome in their home. President Bush was always very supportive of me. We'd sit in his sauna and talk about our families. He was a wonderful man who I could share my thoughts about life. When I got close and got to know him and Barbara, I realized what tremendous, warm, wonderful, genuine and good-hearted people they were.

I never sat in the sauna with Mrs. Bush, but we did spend lots of time sitting in her living room and kitchen. While the other fellas went fishing out on the Atlantic with the President, I sat and talked with Mrs. Bush. During our visits, she shared intimate stories about her kids and what they were going through at the time. Like any other family, they had good times and bad times.

Barbara Bush had a great sense of humor, and she loved to laugh. She also loved my painting, especially the piece I did of her garden. I had prints made of the work, but I gave Mrs. Bush the original. I was honored when my original painting hung in the Bush Presidential Library for more than seven years. It made me proud that someone of their stature appreciated what I did. I also gave them a canvas giclee that looked exactly like the real painting, and just before the Bushes passed away, they gave the original painting back to me.

One August, we were with the Bushes on my mother's birthday. I asked the President if I could use his phone so I could call my mother. Mr. Bush said, "You get her on the phone. I want to wish her a happy birthday." I dialed her number and when she answered, I wished her a Happy Birthday and then I told her there was someone who wanted to say Hi to her. I handed the phone to Mr. Bush, and my mother couldn't believe that he took the time to visit with her. But as I watched the President talk to my mother, I felt that it meant as much to him as it did to her and to me.

The Oak Ridge Boys had a long-term friendship with Mr. and Mrs. Bush that lasted until they both died in 2018. When Mrs. Bush died that April, we attended her funeral in Houston. We sat next to Michael W. Smith and the pro golfer Phil Michelson.

Mr. Bush had always told us that he wanted us to sing at his funeral, and we gave our word that we would. Keeping that word would be quite a challenge.

We were as far out west as we could possibly be when we got word the President had died. We had just kicked off our big Christmas tour, an entire month-long marathon that had us doing one sold-out show every night from Thanksgiving to Christmas.

The night before President's Bush's funeral in Houston, Texas, we were scheduled to perform in Spokane, Washington. We knew if we had to cancel any shows, we'd disappoint thousands of fans and would have to issue tens of thousands of dollars in refunds. But we weren't about to break the promise we'd given to Mr. Bush.

We did the concert in Spokane, as a private plane waited for takeoff at the local airport. As soon as the show ended, we flew all night to Houston. We landed at 5:30 a.m., cleaned up and changed into our suits, and then headed to the church where we sang at the President's funeral.

As we had promised him, we sang Mr. Bush's favorite song, "Amazing Grace." Then, we headed back to the airport and flew across the country, back to Washington state, where we had a concert that night in Kennewick. We got there just in time to walk on stage. We didn't miss a date. But in between those two Washington concerts, we had one hectic trip to Texas. But we had kept our word to our dear friend.

The Oak Ridge Boys have always enjoyed being with the leaders of our country. We've sung for Presidents, senators and congressmen. In 1996, we were asked to sing at a fun event in Washington, D.C. Vermont Senator Jim Jeffords had helped put together a barbershop quartet he called The Singing Senators, and Joe Bonsall's wife Mary saw the Senators on TV singing "Elvira."

The Singing Senators were big fans of the Oak Ridge Boys and we ended up going to Washington to perform with them. We sang patriotic and gospel songs, but as always, it was "Elvira" that brought down the house...or in this case, the Senate. After our performance, it was very late, and Senator Jeffords arranged for us to go to the very top of the dome of Congress. We were the only people up there and I will never forget the sight as we looked out over all the historic sights.

But I would reach much higher heights when I became friends with a true American hero.

General Chuck Yeager was the world's greatest fighter pilot, and he became the first pilot to break the speed of sound. Chuck

Yeager also loved the Oak Ridge Boys. He was as excited to meet us, as we were to meet him…and we were excited! But for over two decades, I became very close friends with Chuck. He and his wife Victoria started coming to our shows, and they would attend at least 3 or 4 of our concerts each year. He would introduce us at dozens of concerts, and I think the crowd was sometimes more excited to see him than us! Chuck also brought many of his pilot buddies to the shows.

General Yeager asked us to attend his 80th birthday party and from that moment, we tried to celebrate his birthday with him each year. Before any show he attended, we would meet backstage and he would share war stories and answer any questions we had. He entertained us and then we'd go out on stage and entertain him.

Chuck took me flying in a variety of different aircraft. He flew me and our tour manager Darrick Kinslow in a helicopter to Barron Hilton's ranch, where he introduced us to a number of NASA astronauts, including Neil Armstrong and Buzz Aldrin. When General Yeager was 85 years old, he took me up in his little Husky plane. It had a pilot seat for the General and one seat directly behind him, where I sat. I have never felt more safe in a plane than I did when Chuck Yeager was behind the controls.

As I was writing this chapter, on December 7, 2020, Chuck Yeager passed away. He was 97 years old. During his time on earth, he had flown higher and faster than just about anyone in the world. Now, he flies even higher.

THE BEARD

"Hey William, how'd you get that beard?"

"I lost my razor."

That's the usual exchange I have when someone on the street yells that question.

For the past four decades, during any interview…every single interview I gave, I was always asked about one thing…my beard. Here are the questions I get the most:

When did you start growing your beard?

Why did you start growing it?

Do you ever trim your beard?

Have you ever thought about shaving it all off?

Has anything funny ever happened because of your beard?

Hopefully, I can answer most of those questions right now…so the interviewers can ask me something else!

I was clean shaven, with no beard of any kind during all our gospel music years. But in the mid-70s, I started to let my beard grow, to where I had a little stubble, a kind of scruffy look. It's the look that most of the guys on the Hallmark Christmas movies have today. I let it grow a little more and started getting compared to Barry Gibb of the Bee Gees.

In November of 1979, we were booked to appear on "The Tonight Show" with Johnny Carson just after Thanksgiving. Dick Howard who worked with Jim Halsey told me, "You need to cut that beard before you go on with Johnny. They don't book rock and roll acts." So, I shaved my beard completely, and I also cut my hair real short. That Christmas, my hair was about as short as it had ever been.

But three weeks later, on January 12, 1980...my 40thbirthday, I looked in the bathroom mirror and said to myself, "I think I will start growing a real beard." By then, Hank Williams, Jr., Charlie Daniels, Waylon Jennings and Willie Nelson all had long beards and longer hair. It also seemed that the longer their hair got, the more success they were having.

From that day on, I just let my beard go. And when I let it go...I let it go. I didn't trim it, and I also didn't cut my hair. After a couple years, my family started to ask when I was going to get a shave and a haircut. My brother and sister both thought I would get tired of it and cut it. My father was always telling me I should "get rid of it and go back to your old look."

As my hair and beard continued to grow, I stopped using the black hair color I had used for years. And the longer my hair and beard got, the greyer they became. It was during that time that I started adopting my "mountain man" persona. Some people called me Grizzly Adams. Many fans didn't know what to make of the major change in my appearance. A lot of them liked it, but many others did not.

I admit that my look went through a wild and wooly period, where I was a little scary looking. I sometimes felt that I was more of a mascot for the group, instead of the baritone singer. But as the years went on, more people began to accept my new look. It really didn't matter to me, if they did or not. I wasn't doing it for them. I was doing it for me.

But over the years, I was a little surprised at what a trademark my beard became. A lot of people compare it to Crystal Gayle's floor-length hair. I think Crystal's hair is pretty cool. I have an idea of what she had to go through to get that trademark, and not many people would be willing to do what she has, to keep her signature hair all these years. I'm sure Crystal also gets some of the same silly questions that I do.

Funny or interesting stories about my beard? Well, I have to be careful around tiki torches, and I've had a number of close calls when I've reached across a table that had candles on it. And I can also make a real mess when I eat biscuits with honey and molasses.

Now that I'm 82 years old, my beard doesn't get any longer. It just gets whiter. Will I ever cut it? I have no plans to. I think it will be with me when I leave this world. I was never tempted to shave over the past 40 years. Many people wanted me to, but as time went on, there were many more people who wanted me to keep it.

When my beard and hair turned white, I started getting called "ZZ Top" quite a bit. Rock fans thought I was one of ZZ Top, but country fans knew who I was. When the TV show "Duck Dynasty" got popular, the Duck Dynasty guys came to Nashville and wanted to meet me. They were known for their beards, but when we stood next to each other, they found that my beard was much longer, but theirs were a little more scruffy. They made me an honorary member of their family.

Jamey Johnson asked me to give him some tips on growing his beard. I explained that most of the length comes from under your chin and not your cheeks. As for caring for my hair and beard...I use Argan Oil on both, and I always like to smell good.

On April 1, 2012, my beard got a lot of attention after our publicist sent out a press release that ended up going around the world. The headline read, "Oak Ridge Boy Member William Lee Golden Makes a Momentous Decision."

The release explained that I had decided to finally cut my hair and beard. It sounded very real, but then took a ridiculous turn as it explained I would be recycling my hair to use it to make my paint brushes. At the time, I was getting recognized for my paintings, and the press release quoted me saying, "I wanted to add a little more of myself into each painting."

Our publicists figured everyone would know the release was a complete joke…especially since it was sent out on April 1st…April Fool's Day! But quite a few radio DJs, newspaper outlets and TV stations ran the story as if it were totally real. I got so many emails, messages, letters and calls from heartbroken fans who were mourning the death of my beard!

In 2017, my son Craig started growing out his beard. And by 2020, he looked almost exactly like me. His beard is impressive, and he looks good with it. When people see Craig, they sometimes think he's me. And when I'm scrolling through social media, I sometimes get a quick glimpse of a picture of him, and I think it's me.

During the pandemic, I listened to everyone complain that they couldn't go to the beauty shop or barber shop. I didn't have to worry about that. I hadn't paid for a haircut or shave in over 40 years!

I feel very comfortable with my beard. I would be lost without it today. I like to say, "It's part of me and I got attached to it. But it's actually attached to me."

THE MAN IN BLACK DIES AND GOLDEN COMES CLOSE

On May 19, 2003, we sang goodbye to June Carter Cash. June's husband Johnny asked us to sing, "Loving God, Loving Each Other" at June's funeral service at the First Baptist Church in Hendersonville. The church is located less than a mile from Johnny and June's home.

Less than four months later, we gathered in that same church for Johnny's funeral. If someone could ever die of a broken heart, Johnny did. As I sat through the many tributes to Johnny, I realized just how fast time flies by. So many memories of my time with John flooded through my mind. I smiled as I thought of how fortunate the Oaks were to have been a part of Johnny Cash's show, and for him to be such an important part of our lives.

I remembered what a true friend he was when I was out of the group. He had invited me over and we talked about the past and our dreams for the future. Talking to Johnny Cash was kind of like talking to a President…but Johnny had more power.

I came close to joining Johnny and June in Heaven's choir less than a year later.

On August 7, 2004, I was out walking like I try to do each day. We had played a show the night before in Wausaw, Wisconsin. Since we had a rare day off, we planned to stay in town and then leave the next night. I went walking in Wausaw that afternoon, but as I walked, something didn't feel right in my chest. At one point, I had to stop walking and rest for a minute. I turned around and headed toward our bus, but before I got there, I had to stop again.

I didn't have any pain, but instead, I had a weird feeling in my chest. When I finally reached the bus, I sat down, and again, the odd feeling came over me. I knew that something wasn't right. I tried to eat a little bit, but I felt nauseous. When I lost my appetite, I asked them to take me to the hospital, so I could get checked out.

I walked into the emergency room, and they hooked me up to an EKG machine. A doctor came in to talk to me, and I told him I was starting to get the same weird feeling in my chest again. He looked at the live EKG reading and said, "It looks like you are about to have a heart attack."

I told him, "Our bus is going to leave town at midnight." The doctor replied, "Well, you're not going to be on it. You are very close to having a Widow Maker attack. If you hadn't come in when you did, you would have left Wisconsin in a hearse."

The main artery in my heart was 95% blocked. The doctor said if I would have had that heart attack on the bus, I would not have made it to the hospital. They operated immediately and ran a line from my groin up to my heart, so they could put in a stent. When I came to, I could instantly feel a difference. I was up walking the next day, with no damage to my heart.

While I recovered, Jimmy Fulbright and my son Chris filled in for me on the Oaks' concerts for a couple months. Chris called me and said, "Dad, they put a sign in the lobby before the show. It said, 'Tonight, Chris Golden will be singing for his father William Lee.' Thankfully, no one asked for their money back."

This book would have never happened if I had put off going to the hospital when I had that weird feeling in my chest. If I had stayed on the bus and left town at midnight, I wouldn't be here today.

Now, almost 17 years later, I go every six months to get a check-up with Doctor David Hansen, the director of cardiology at Vanderbilt. Ironically, Dr. Hansen majored in music in college. He wanted to be the leader of a symphony orchestra, but he ended up going into the medical field. He's still a wonderful piano player, and he is still involved in music a little…as he helps keep me alive.

I started this chapter off with the death of Johnny Cash. A few years after "The Man in Black" died, there was another huge loss for Johnny's family, friends and fans. I was at home on the afternoon of April 9, 2007, and I could see a huge amount of smoke coming from the Old Hickory Lake area, about 5 miles from my house. It looked like it was near Johnny's home.

Barry Gibb, one of the famous Bee Gees had recently purchased Johnny and June's historic home. I had become close friends with Barry, and I had visited with him just a few days before. He told me how he was looking forward to moving to Nashville to become a part of our music community. Barry was excited about living in Johnny's former home and had been busy having the estate refurbished. He explained that the work was almost complete, just as soon as the workers put the finishing touches on everything.

As the smoke continued to billow, I got my wife and son Solomon, and we drove toward the blaze. As we got closer, I kept hoping that it wasn't Johnny's home. But it was.

One of the workers had been shellacking some flooring. They were smoking a cigarette while they worked, and they accidently set that shellack on fire. The entire house was built totally out of wood and logs, and it went up in no time. My family watched as Johnny Cash's home burned to the ground. It was exactly one year and 2 days since the tornado had destroyed my own home. I guess the lesson in all this is: If you're going to be a country music star…you need to have a good homeowner's insurance policy.

The Soaked Ridge Boy. Photo by Mary Master-Martin

With my parents in Brewton. Photo by Alan Messer

The Oaks singing backup for Charlie Daniels at my Harvest Jam.
Photo by Carol Pate Baker

Yes, a few people turned out for my Harvest Jam in my hometown of Brewton, Alabama. Photo by Alan Messer.

Getting a hug from my father during Harvest Jam.

An Oaks photo shoot, 1982. Photo by Alan Messer.

Joe doing his best Weird Al impression.
Photo by Alan Messer

In 1982, Alan Messer created this wonderful peice of art. Yes, we really were outside and I was on a real horse!

Performing to another sold out crowd.
Photo by Alan Messer.

On our American Made tour, 1983. Photo by Alan Messer

Promoting our Christmas album. Photo by Alan Messer

The Oaks in Reno, Nevada. Photo by Alan Messer

The Oaks and our manager, mentor and friend Jim Halsey, 1985.
Photo by Alan Messer

I'm sure Joe has wanted to kick me in the rear a few times!
Photos by Carol Pate Baker

The fans always want a photo of the four of us close together.

July 1984. Photos by Mary Master-Martin

Duane, I swear I thought it was casual Friday!

Recording in Elvis' home-
town of Memphis.
Photo by Alan Messer

Alan Messer contact
sheet as Booker T. Jones
produces my American
Vagabond album.

Harrah's, Lake Tahoe, 1985. Photo by Alan Messer

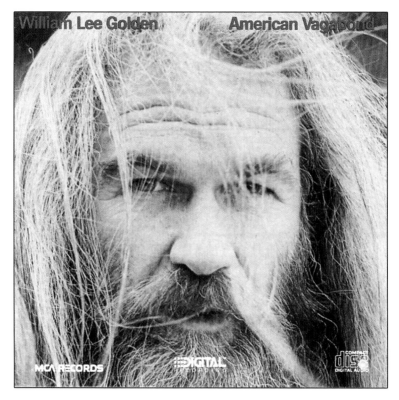

My 1986 solo album. Alan Messer shot the album cover.

Enjoying a ballgame with my second wife Luetta, 1985.
Photo by Alan Messer

Visiting with my mother and father in the kitchen of my childhood home.
Photo by Alan Messer

A family get-together with my brother, sister and mother.

On stage with Steve
Sanders at the
Indiana State Fair.
Aug. 1986.

I love getting close
to our fans at the
Kentucky State Fair.
Aug. 1986

My first solo concert with The Goldens on Nov. 14, 1987.

gning autographs with Rusty and hris at Nashville orth, Taylorville, inois. Photos by Anne Pate

With Chris and Rusty, The Goldens.
Photo by Alan Messer

In Reno, Nevada, 1986. Photo by Alan Messer

May, 1989. Photo by Alan Messer

On stage with the legendary George Jor
May 1989. Photos by Alan Messe

Driving the bus for the Goldens.
Photo by Anne Pate

Chopping wood at my home on New Year's Day, 1988.
Photo by Carol Pate Baker

On the road in Cleveland, Ohio.

With Linda Moore,
Feb. 1988.
Photos by Anne Pate

Cooking with my son Chris for a Golden Fan Club party.
Photo by Anne Pat[

Doing all the cooking during a party for my fans.
Photo by Carol Pate Baker

May 1989. Photo by Anne Pate

With my son Chris at a Fan Fair event. Photo by Carol Baker

The Goldens, 1989
(Back row L-R) John
Rich, Rusty, Chris,
Greg Gordon, Don
Breland. (Bottom L-R)
Skip Mitchell, William,
John Sturdivant, Jr.

William and Brenda
engagement picture.
The Oak Ridge Boys'
bass player Don
Breland took the
photo.

Signing autographs at Fan Fair.

Keep Lookin' Up.
Charlotte, NC.
Photos by Anne Pate

Performing with The Goldens at the Bell Cove Club in Hendersonville, TN.

On stage at Ponderosa Park, Salem, Ohio.
Photo by Anne Pate

A new dad at the age of 62! With my baby boy Solomon.

First steps with my son Solomon.

Some of the crowd that came out for the tour and blessing of our renovated home. Photo by Anne Pate

My friend Richard Brown spends Thanksgiving at our home. You can read about Richard in the chapter A Tale of Two Friends.

A rare photo with all four of my sons, Chris, Solomon, Craig and Rusty. My great niece Emma is on the right. Photo by Alan Messer

Yes, it's really me! Showing off the phot the other Oaks signed for their fan. You can read the story in the Brenda and Solomon chapter.

My son Solomon joins me for the opening of my art exhibit at the BNA airport.
Photo by Anne Pate

Introducing Solomon to Kenny Rogers.

Thank God for kids.
Solomon joins me
on stage.
Photo by
Anne Pate

Getting baptized at Mt Zion Baptist Church in Nashville.

With Solomon after my baptisim.

With Solomon in front of Big Ben in London.

Little Jimmy Dickens invites the Oaks to become Opry members.

Presenting my painting of the Bush Garden to President George H.W
and Barbara Bush.

With my son Chris and ex-wife Frogene. Branson, Missouri, 2002.
Photo by Anne Pate

With my grandson
Elijah on stage at
Renfro Valley.
Photo by Anne Pate

I admit that my hair and beard can get a little out of place...especially during a strong wind! Photos by Anne Pate

Jeff Panzer has been my best friend for over 40 years. Anne Pate took the top photo shortly after our friendship began.

annefrancespate

Jeff hasn't chang
much in 4 decad
but my beard an
hair have gotten
longer and greye

If it's showtime...don't get in the way! Photo by Ron Fairchild

I was honored with a special showing of my paintings at the Pensacola Museum of Art. My neice, Dana is next to me in the black top.

My friend Phil Johnson took this photo of me when I appeared on
Larry's Country Diner.

Singing (and serving) on the Larry's Country Diner TV show.
Photos by Phil Johnson

Renae Johnson gives me tips on
how to be the perfect waitress.
Photo by Jayne England

General Chuck Yeager was a true American hero. He also loved the Oak Ridge Boys!

The Oaks with 3 men who were so important to us. Sherman Halsey, Jim Halsey and Jim Foglesong. Photo by Jon Mir.

Performing at the
Riverside Resort.

Photos by
Anne Pate

With Oak Ridge Boy
superfan Mary Wheat.

04/18/2008

With our fear friend Kenny Rogers during our Country Music Hall of Fame induction ceremony. Jody Williams, from the Hall of Fame is on the left.

Backstage with my friends Sylvia and Charley Pride.

Along Route 66 outside Laughlin, NV. Photo by Cathy Barnes

The world's worst speedboat driver!

This small photo on the right captured the first time I met Simone. 35 years later, she would become my wife.
Photo by Karen Cachopo.

William and Simone's wedding day.

With Simone in Laughlin, Nevada.

With Simone in
Pueblo, Colorado
Photo by Louis
Stephenson

With my sons Craig, Rusty and Chris. Photo by Michael Jenkins

I love to welcome friends to my home. Photo by Jerry Overcast

Simone and I make the cover of the Hendersonville Lifestyles magazin

Returning to the fields where I spent my youth and teen years in Brewton, AL. Photos by Michael Jenkins

I've taken hundreds of photos
of Simone. These
are a few of my favorites.

With Craig and Rusty. Photo by Michael Jenkins

At the 2018 Music City Bowl game with my son Solomon

Attending Don Breland's memorial service with Duane Allen and Tony Brown. Photo by Alan Messer.

Paying respects to my parents. Photo by Michael Jenkins

Recreating Norman Rockwell's American Gothic with Ron Fairchild, in Eldon, Iowa.

Always looking for the perfect sunset.
Photo by Chris Golden

My son Chris took this photo of me with the guitar my father gave me when I was 11 years old.

Going on a walk with my dog Sampson. Photo by Alan Messer

Looking back at one of my first videos as an Oak Ridge Boy.
Photo by Michael Jenkins

Rusty plays piano as we rehearse in my living room.

In the studio with my friend Michael Sykes.
Photos by Michael Jenkins

With Chris and Rusty.

Enjoying my son Craig as we record our new music.
Photos by Michael Jenkins

Enjoying an Orange Beach Alabama sunset with Simone.

Simone and I celebrate our 4th wedding anniversary.

With Simone in our little house in Burns, Tennessee.

My heart is full when my home is full of my children, grandchildren and great grandchildren.

Thank God for kids, grandkids and great grandkids too.

With 3 great grandkids. Elayna Kye, Imogen. Dec. 12, 2020

Alan Messer took this photo of me taking a photo as a storm rolled in.

Celebrating my 81st birthday. Photo by Alan Messer

My friend Michael Jenkins wanted to try to "capture my cool".
This was the best I could do.

THE FANS

"William has a relationship with the fans that no other entertainer has. I have been with him for 200 to 300 days a year for 40 years, and I've never once seen him turn down someone who was waiting for an autograph, a picture or handshake. He will always take time to visit with people. He doesn't do that out of a sense of duty. He does it because he genuinely loves meeting people. He does it every day. I watch the way he relates to fans and it is very special to watch. I wish I could treat people as good as he does, and I try to, but there is only one William Lee."

— Richard Sterban

I thank Richard for his kind words. All the Oaks have tried to pay back the fans in their own way over the years.

Duane stays close to our fans via social media. He's always on the computer and very active on all of our Twitter, Facebook and other social media pages. He takes care of fans' questions and keeps them up-to-date on everything that's happening with us. Joe is also quite accessible to fans on the internet. Joe and Richard also get close to our fans through the many radio, TV and newspaper interviews they do.

During our concerts, Joe is the one who does most of the talking to the audience. I like to keep up my "strong and silent" image! Joe has a gift for being quick on his feet during our shows, and he can handle anything that comes up. More than a few times, someone has gotten sick in the audience, (hopefully, not from my singing) and they've had to bring in emergency crews to take them out. Joe always handles each situation in a very professional and personal way. It's not easy to watch a fan be carried out on a stretcher, and then you have to go back into singing "Elvira."

On stage, we've always wanted to make sure we are giving the fans all that we've got. Every day and every show, we try to give them our very best. And over the decades, me, Richard, Joe and Duane have posed for tens of thousands of photos and signed even more autographs for our fans.

The word 'fan' is short for fanatic. Sports teams have fanatical fans, and if we're lucky, even country music stars can have a few of those. When some sports teams have to suffer through losing years, and terrible seasons, their fans will suffer along with them, and they keep cheering them on until they finally win. It's the same way when a musical artist is not having any hits, or is not drawing very big crowds. But they still have loyal fans who will cheer them on through the bad times, in hopes of bigger success the next year.

We are sincerely grateful for all our fans, whether you bought one CD or have our entire collection of albums, cassettes, and 8-tracks! If you've been to one concert, we thank you. If you've been to 500 concerts, we are humbled that you would give up such a large part of your life to cheer us on.

One of our super fans is Jane King. She's a pastry chef from St. Louis, who has attended more than 500 of our concerts. There are many others who we have seen at show after show. It makes our day to see them. We know when they're in the crowd, they'll pass their excitement and enthusiasm on to the people around them, and we'll be in for a fun night.

Our oldest fan was Una Reeks. We called her Aunt Una. She lived to be 105, and I think she attended her last Oaks show when she was 104. She became part of our family as she came to hundreds of concerts. Now, her daughter, Mary Wheat has taken up where Aunt Una left off. I have no idea how many shows Mary has attended, but it's several hundred.

Anne Pate and her twin sister Carol were two of our most loyal fans over the years. I'm pretty sure that they attended more concerts than anyone else. Anne still comes to lots of our shows, but Carol passed away a couple years ago.

Anne's family came to see us for the first time almost 40 years ago. I met her mother and Anne and Carol. They were identical twins, and since my dad was a triplet, I could relate to them. Over the years, Anne became more than a fan. She became a true friend.

I don't know of many other artists who would give one of their fans the chance to be a part of their autobiography, but I wanted to ask Anne if all the time, miles and tickets she bought was worth it. Here's her answer:

"My sister Carol and I were very, very shy. We were raised in rural North Carolina, and we didn't get to go to a lot of live concerts. In 1979, Daddy asked us if we wanted to see the Oak Ridge Boys in Fayetteville. We didn't know much about them, but we said yes.

Our seats were pretty far away, but we took turns walking down front to take photos. Carol went first, and as she was taking photos, Duane pointed to her, and she fell instantly in love with him. When she came back to her seat, she said, "Anne, you need to go down and pick out which one you like. But that good looking one pointed to me, and he's mine!" I went down and took a good look at all of them. When I came back, I announced to Carol, "I like Bill."

Carol and I were 22 years old, but we looked about 15 and we were very introverted and naïve. Our daddy was very shy, so we got it from him. But when he saw us out, having fun at the Oaks concert, he liked it, so he kept taking us to shows. Our second Oaks concert was in March of 1980 in Greensboro. Daddy loaded us all up in the station wagon. We also saw them at Busch Gardens.

In June of 1980, we went to Fan Fair, where we attended the Oak Ridge Boys' Fan Open House. It was the first time we met the group. Little did I know that I would eventually help run William's fan club booth at Fan Fair. The next month, we saw them at another concert and our entire family met them.

In February of 1981, our daddy was killed in a wreck. Since he had been the one who had bought our first Oaks tickets, and since he was so happy to see us "come out of our shells" when we were at the Oaks' shows, Carol and I thought we should go to another concert, in honor of our dad. When we got there, we felt such a feeling of peace and healing. For a couple hours, we didn't feel the pain of losing our father.

I have no idea how many Oaks shows I've attended since then. I don't know if it's a thousand, but for sure, it's in the high hundreds.

On October 17, 1982, Carol and I were waiting by the Oak's bus in Wilmington, North Carolina. William walked off the bus and told us he was going to do a new song that night. That song was "Thank God for Kids." He got a standing ovation. I could tell that it humbled him so much that he didn't know what to say. It was a defining moment.

I think "Thank God for Kids" was just as important as "Elvira" and "Bobbie Sue." "Thank God for Kids" has a message, and the fans all want him to sing it. I think it should be in every concert they do. Of course, when he recorded "Little Annie's Christmas Wish," that also became a favorite of mine, since it had my name in the title.

The Oaks played a show in Massachusetts, and we had to drive right through the middle of New York City to get there. We followed their bus through the city, and we never stopped or tried to see any of the sights of the Big Apple. We just drove through New York so we could get to the Oaks.

They were playing the Westbury Music Fair on our birthday. The show was in the round, with a rotating stage. During the concert, William called Carol up on stage and he whispered, "Happy Birthday." Then he called me up on stage and did the same thing.

When William was asked to leave the group, that really hurt us too. We were hurt and also angry. I was so mad that I once caught Joe in a parking lot and I told him off. I really gave it to him. I'm sorry Joe! I know he forgives me. I forgive him too. There is great power in forgiveness. Forgiveness makes everyone's life so much easier and better.

During the 9 years he was away from the group, we had a lot of fun as fans of The Goldens. It allowed us to get closer to William and spend more time with him, and at a lot their concerts, we got to hear William sing all night long.

When the Oaks asked William to come back, I was so happy. I was actually in the audience the night he made his return. William had called me a month before to tell me he thought it was going to happen. Then his wife Brenda called me to tell me I should spend New Year's

Eve in Merrillville, Indiana. We drove from North Carolina to Indiana to see William rejoin the Oaks. It was a night I will remember for as long as I live.

Our love for William and the Oak Ridge Boys helped us get to know so many people I would have never met. I have made a lot of "Golden Friends" over the years. One of those was Linda Moore. We met at a show and became like sisters. I think Carol, Linda and I were the number one William fans. We all had a special bond with him. He always knew we had his back, and we were there for him. He knew we cared about him as a person.

William is just a sweet, wonderful person. He has given happiness to so many people. He gives a lot of love out to people who he doesn't even know. He gave me, Carol and Linda so much happiness. Linda died in 2013. With Carol also gone, now I have to go to the concerts by myself. But it doesn't take me long to make friends with the people I'm sitting next to.

If I hadn't become such a fan of the Oak Ridge Boys, I would have missed out on so much fun. I'm sure my dad would be happily surprised at what he started when he took me to that first Oaks show. I'm sure he would love it."

— Anne Pate

I know my fans love me, and I love them back. I'm a fan too. There are many artists that I'm a fan of. If you love an artist, the last thing you want is to find out that they are a real jerk. If you get to meet them and they are not what you imagine they will be, it can be a major letdown. I have occasionally seen some artists be rude to fans who come up to them.

I was with an artist and we were having dinner at a restaurant. I won't say who it was, but I watched them be very rude to a fan. A woman came up and politely asked for an autograph and he said, "I will sign your autograph when I'm done having my meal." When we were done, he went to the woman and she told him she didn't want his autograph anymore. He ended up almost forcing it on her, but it was too late. It only takes a moment to lose a fan forever.

I always felt that if a fan approaches you, they might think this is the one and only time they will have to take a photo or get an autograph. So, even if I'm eating, I have never minded stopping to take a photo or saying "Hi" or signing an autograph. If you are eating a meal at home, you probably jump up a few times to get something, so when I'm out, it was never a hassle to me to stop for a second or two.

I try to walk every day. I am pretty recognizable and I get stopped almost every time I go out. People ask if they can take a photo, and I don't mind at all. That's part of it. If you're an entertainer, you shouldn't mind when fans approach you. If you do, then why in the heck did you get in the business in the first place?

The fans take time to come to our concerts. They go to great expense and drive long distances to see us. They take off work and pay for hotel rooms, in addition to buying the concert tickets. I want to make sure we give them their money's worth, and that we live up to their image of us. If we get to meet in person, by the bus or at the hotel or when I'm out walking, I try to treat everybody right.

When I'm meeting fans after a concert, you'll usually see our tour manager Darrick Kinslow close by me. He's the man who is always looking at his watch! One of Darrick's many duties is to make sure we get to our next date on time. He started with us many years ago, as a fill-in bus driver. Timmer Ground had been with us for 25 years, and when he left to take care of his wife, I knew finding someone as great as him would not be easy. But as I watched Darrick go above and beyond in his job,

I thought he would make the perfect tour manager. I fought for him to get the job, and he has been great.

Since Darrick is always close by all of us when we're on tour, it's also important that he has the same respect for the fans that Joe, Duane, Richard and I have. Even when he's trying to get me on the bus, Darrick always treats our fans with patience and kindness.

Richard, Duane, Joe and I never got in this business for a one-time deal. We wanted to go back to play the same places time and time again. If we did a show and the fans didn't show up, that would be a sad day. I want to make sure that day never comes.

A TALE OF TWO FRIENDS

I'd like to tell you about a couple of my friends. One went from being a big Oak Ridge Boys fan to becoming our record producer, and eventually he would fill in for me in concert. My other friend drove a chicken truck.

Michael Sykes was 11 years old when he attended his first Oak Ridge Boys concert. We were his introduction to four-part harmony. Today, Michael is a very popular gospel singer, musician, songwriter, and producer. I'm honored he took time out of his busy schedule to share a few words in my book:

> "When I heard the Oak Ridge Boys in 1969, they inspired me. When I saw them in concert, it was a true life-changing moment for me. I knew what I was going to do for the rest of my life. I was going to work in the music business in some way.
>
> The Oak Ridge Boys were bigger than life to me. Watching William, I realized that he is not a Pavarotti type singer. He's not a Kenny Rogers, but he's a stylist all his own. He can interpret and sell a song like nobody else. He gave me hope that I could do that, and he made me know that if I was determined enough, I could find a way to make my own mark in the music business.
>
> In 2001, I was working for Springhill Music and I thought I could do a great record on the Oaks. It was a dream that I figured would never come true. But I was

able to help sign the Oaks to our label, and they sang some things that blew me away. I was producer on their "From the Heart" album, which won a Gospel Music Dove Award for the Oaks, and I went on to produce quite a few albums for them.

Golden is one of a kind. He is iconic, and there is no one else like him. He can't go anywhere without people recognizing him, and he's totally fine with that. But he's always been the same, and has never changed, no matter how much success he has achieved.

Over the years, William has become one of my dearest friends. He is a giver, not a taker. He's one of the most generous guys I've ever met. There was a man on Music Row. His name was Richard, and he was autistic. Richard didn't have a way around and William asked the other Oaks and me to chip in so we could buy him a car. William's brother had a car dealership, and he helped us get a nice used car, and when we gave it to Richard, you would have thought we had given him a brand-new Rolls Royce.

William is probably the most honest person I've ever met. He is probably too honest at times, but he will tell the truth even if it hurts him, and if he tells you the sky is falling, you'd better be looking up, because the sky is coming down. William has so much integrity. I love the ground he walks on, and I count him as a brother."

— Michael Sykes

Michael mentioned my friend Richard Brown. I called him Little Richard, and he was an interesting guy. He was originally from Connecticut, and he was a big fan of the Oak Ridge Boys, going back to our gospel days. He'd come to our concerts and he'd get there before we did. Richard drove a big chicken truck that had crates of live chickens in the back. We'd pull into the church we were playing, and we'd see that chicken truck in the parking lot, and we'd know Richard was there.

Richard loved the all-night singings we did in Harrisburg, and he'd sit on the front row with his dog that was named Rawhide. His dog was his best friend. Richard was autistic, but back then, no one understood what that meant, so Richard was subject to a lot of unkind treatment. People also judged him on his outward appearance and didn't take the time to get to know how intelligent he truly was.

Richard was similar to the movie character Rain Man. He was a brilliant little guy, who had a photographic memory. He got the highest grades of anyone in his school. He knew every road in America, and he had also memorized every radio station in the country. He could recite their call letters and tell you where they were. He could also name every state capitol.

I hired Richard to drive an equipment truck for us. He was very dependable, and he had a great heart. Richard moved to Nashville and lived in a low-income apartment. People would see him walking down Music Row and think he was homeless. He didn't have any family, but he had me. I would occasionally bring him home with me. My kids got to know him, and I'd have him at our home for Thanksgiving.

Richard knew Joe Bonsall before Joe joined the Oaks. Richard attended concerts by Joe's Keystone Quartet. Joe has these memories of him:

> "Richard Brown was a savant. Most people saw him as mentally disabled, but he could tell you the population of every major city in the country. People didn't know what to think of him, but the one person who understood him more than anyone else was William Lee Golden.
>
> Richard loved gospel music, and I heard he had one of the greatest gospel music record collections in the world. He followed our Keystone Quartet, and drove his chicken

truck to our shows. One time, Richard was driving through downtown Boston, and he crashed his truck in the downtown tunnel. There were chickens everywhere in that tunnel.

We were going to tour Sweden and Richard wanted to drive our truck to Sweden. William had to explain to him that you can't drive to Sweden. When Richard moved to Nashville, people would see him walking the streets, looking in trash cans. He was dirty and sometimes smelled like a chicken truck, long after his chicken days were over. Some people jokingly referred to him as "The Mayor of Music Row."

While others would laugh, Golden really looked after Richard. He took him to his own home, gave him a shower and cleaned him up. I know William also gave him money, in addition to the car we gave him. I visited with Richard numerous times, but I really got to know him when I started seeing him through the eyes of William Lee Golden."

– Joe Bonsall

When I heard Richard was in the hospital, near death, I went to visit him. We were true friends, and I know that he appreciated our relationship. But I'm sure that I got more out of our friendship than he did.

LOSING EVERYTHING

I'm happy to say that I was a much better husband during my third marriage. I wasn't perfect, but I did my very best. Brenda and I had more than two decades of great times together. We also had a few stormy times…and not just the day the tornado rolled through our house.

Everything was fine in our marriage…until it went bad. There was no big "last straw" that ended our marriage, just a lot of small things that eventually added up to unhappiness.

In 2012, we took a trip to London. From there, we rode a train under the English Channel to Paris. I was happy to take our 10-year-old son Solomon with us. While we were there, I had a feeling that something was going to change. Brenda might have been feeling that too. But as we enjoyed our family vacation, I told myself, "You should savor this moment." I had a strange, haunting feeling, a premonition that we would never repeat this special time together.

Later that year, while I was out with the Oaks on our Christmas tour, Brenda told Solomon that we were going to get a divorce and they would be moving out. He cried all night. As soon as our Christmas tour was over, I came home, and we all headed to Disney World. It would be our last family vacation. Brenda and I did it for Solomon, but we ended up putting him in an awkward position.

I have always said that people should not stay where they don't want to be. Brenda took me up on that in January of 2013. I was served divorce papers. I got my travel bag and moved into our little cabin next door. Brenda continued to live in our main house, and I was just a few feet across our yard for the next year and a half. I didn't mind staying in the cabin. I never needed a big fancy place to be happy. I can live in a teepee and be at peace.

But finding peace would not be easy as our mostly pleasant marriage quickly turned into a very bitter divorce. It was heartbreaking and disappointing to go through such a painful divorce. It turned into a nightmare for everyone…a nightmare that I didn't wake up from for many years.

I tried to keep my heartache to myself and not "bring it to work." It was 2 months after being served with divorce papers, that I finally mentioned it to the other Oak Ridge Boys.

A year and a half after being served papers, our divorce proceedings were still dragging on. For one reason…so a lot of lawyers could get rich. I was ready to take a hammer to one of my own lawyers. The lawyers just bleed everybody dry. If they keep both sides fighting, they can keep adding hours to their fee.

After one of Brenda's lawyers sent me a threatening letter, when I saw him in person, I told him, "You are going to have to back up your words right now. Don't you ever threaten me." All my lawyers held me back from taking his head off.

At another contentious meeting with a room full of attorneys, they forced me to put my home and all of "Golden Era" up for sale. While I was out on tour, the locks to the home were all changed. I felt helpless. I had bought the place when I was a bachelor, and now I was locked out. I could look in the windows and see all my gold records still hanging on the wall.

Some of my friends said, "You ought to break in and go get your stuff." Others said, "Just take a sledgehammer and destroy everything, and then there won't be anything for her to take." But I would never have done that. I loved "Golden Era," and I would never break a window or door to get inside. The last thing I would have wanted was to make a big scene by breaking into my own home.

About six months into the long, sad process, it became apparent that our divorce would not become final anytime in the near, or not so near future. I told the lawyers, "Guys, I'm 73 years old, and you are going to drag this out until I die. I want to move forward with my life." I told my lawyers that I was going to start dating someone (the woman who would eventually become my wife.) My lawyer said, "Oh, Mr. Golden, as your lawyer, I have to advise you to not do that. The other side will use it to take everything you have." I asked, "You want me to sit around and waste my life, so you can live yours as you use my money?"

Then I really gave my lawyers a piece of my mind as I said, "I really didn't give a damn what the judge thinks about me moving on with my life. As far as I'm concerned, my marriage was over the day I was served with divorce papers. Not one time in my life have I asked a judge if I could go on a date, and I'm damn sure not going to start now."

By the time the divorce was final, I had lost my home. I had lost all my property. I had lost all my money…almost every cent. And most importantly, I had lost my son. I could handle losing everything else, but not being able to be with my son was completely heart wrenching. I knew that Solomon needed a father in his life, and I worried about how us being apart would affect him.

I had made a lot of mistakes in my life. I've certainly paid a price for them too. The mental, emotional, physical and spiritual costs I've paid are so high. But I needed to move on. I knew that Brenda did too. I tried to use the horrible experience as a challenge that I needed to rise above and move forward.

My awards, framed platinum records, photos and other memorabilia were all boxed up and taken to a storage facility. I moved to Burns, Tennessee, where my friend Gary Spicer allowed me to live in his little farmhouse in Burns almost rent free. He charged me just $100 a month.

My home of 30 years, "Golden Era" was put up for sale. It stayed on the market for two years. Finally, after I met with my new lawyers Terry and Debrah Frizzell and my long-time friend and lawyer Wayne Halper, they both said, "William, why don't you buy back "Golden Era" yourself? You need to be in that house."

I can honestly say my third divorce was the most stressful time of my life. It was even more stressful than when I was fired by the Oaks. I don't know if divorces have ever made a person better, but they can sure make you wiser. With each experience, good or bad, I've tried to learn, grow and become a better person.

I WAS CREATED TO CREATE

For eight decades, I have been in awe and wonder of the world we live in. I especially love beautiful landscapes and historical places. Over the past 20 years, I've tried to capture some of that beauty through my love of painting and photography.

During my travels with the Oak Ridge Boys, and on my personal vacations, I've enjoyed visiting many of the world's great museums and art galleries. I'm always in awe when I get to see the authentic and priceless works of the true masters.

The Christmas after my son Solomon was born, there was a huge present under our tree. When I opened it Christmas morning, there was an easel, some canvases, brushes and paints. There was a card with it that said, "Merry Christmas Daddy. Now paint us a painting. Solomon and Brenda." It really touched my heart. I was inspired to create something that would be there for Solomon after I was gone. I wanted to do something that he could remember me by.

I watched instructional videos to educate myself about painting, and I also studied legendary painters. I learned how they mixed and applied their paint. My paintings are layered with many different colors. I really take my time on each flower and tree to get the light and color exactly right. One tree might have 6 or 7 different shades of green. I was such a slow painter, and I got aggravated with myself because I was so slow. Each of my paintings would take me 6 months to complete.

My first painting was some hay bales down at the creek at the end of my yard. For my second piece, I traveled back to our old farm in Alabama and I painted some azaleas there. I eventually advanced from our hometown azaleas to Monet's garden. I visited the great Claude Monet's home in Giverny, France a couple times, and one of my most popular works is one I painted of Monet's garden.

I did most of my paintings on the road. We'd store all my canvases, easel, and painting gear in the bay under our tour bus. When we would get to a new town, I'd roll everything up to my hotel room. I'd set up my supplies by the window, and I also carried lights with me in case it was a cloudy day. I'd hang the lights on the hotel curtains, and I turned my hotel room into a real art studio.

I found comfort and joy in painting. It gave me something productive to do on the road. Rather than sitting in a hotel room, watching TV all day, I'd try to get out early and take a walk, and then come back and paint until showtime.

Someone told me that Picasso once said, "Painting is just another way of keeping a diary." And that's exactly what it was for me. All my paintings were of places I had been. When I saw a location that touched me, I'd take a picture and then eventually turn that photo into a painting. Each piece would become a diary-like memory for me, and the locations ranged from the creek just outside my home to the Superstition Mountains in Arizona

When I was painting, I really poured myself into buying books on art and going to art museums. I love the impressionist painters. I also became friends with David Wright, an incredible frontier painter.

When I walk by one of my paintings, it gives me a feeling of comfort because I remember all the hours I had spent in front of that canvas. Today, I am humbled when I think of the thousands of people who have admired my paintings. I was asked to display my work in a special exhibit at the Nashville International Airport. It was supposed to run 3 months, but it was extended to 6, and then again to 10 months. During that time, as millions of tourists flew into Nashville, my paintings were the very first thing they saw as soon as they got off the plane.

I had a big showing at the Pensacola Art Museum, and the Tennessee State Museum in Nashville displayed 23 of my paintings. I own all my originals except the one I donated to the Tennessee State Museum.

I painted for a dozen years, but I have not picked up a brush since 2013. To be honest, I kind of lost confidence in my painting. When I went through the divorce, the lawyers wanted me to put a value on all my paintings. They wanted to know what my art was worth. I had never done it to sell, and I've never sold any of my originals. I did it to create a work of art. When we started haggling over what my paintings were worth and how to divide them, it really destroyed my passion for painting.

But when I stopped painting, I found another talent. I started taking pictures.

I actually got into photography when I started painting. I would pass a scene and say, "That would make a beautiful painting." I'd take a photo with a cheap camera and when I'd get them developed, they were nothing like I had been looking at.

Things changed when I started taking digital photos in 2008. Just before my mother passed away, I got more serious about photography, and about my cameras, so I could have a good quality picture and better reference to paint from. I admire "real" photographers, and I got lots of great advice from my friend Jimmy Moore, who took a lot of the early Oak Ridge Boys photos.

One of my favorite things to photograph are sunsets. I've always loved sunsets. I love sunrises too, but they seem to come too early for me! I've taken thousands of sunset shots, and each one is different. I call the 30 minutes before and after sunset, "The Golden Hour." I've photographed sunsets in the deserts of the Southwest, The Grand Canyon, Old Hickory Lake in Hendersonville, Tennessee and hundreds at my family farm in Alabama.

In addition to my paintings, I have been blessed to have been asked to display some of my photography. I had a big showing at the Pensacola airport, and a 2-month exhibit at the Monthaven Art Center in our home of Hendersonville, Tennessee.

I wish I had started my photography earlier in life. It is one of my true loves. I've been known to go to great lengths to capture the perfect photo. I've gotten close to some dangerous places, like out on a rocky ledge of a rugged cliff above the Pacific Ocean. It was straight down, and I knew a strong gust of wind would blow me over the side.

To get just the right picture, I ventured out on the very edge of the Grand Canyon. As I look at the photos now, I know I got too close to the edge. A rock giving way would have been the end of me. It was a long way down. I've tried to cut back on some of my more precarious adventures. Sunsets are a lot less dangerous!

I have lived my life trying to be an artist in music and in art and photography. Hopefully, through one of those forms, I have been able to bring some joy and happiness to a few people. To see some of my paintings and photographs you can visit my website at www.williamleegolden.com.

COUNTRY'S HIGHEST HONOR

In the winter of 2015, we were playing the Grand Ole Opry. Our manager Jim Halsey was with us, and just before we walked out to perform, he told us we needed to have a meeting in our dressing room after our performance. We didn't think much of it, since Jim always had some new idea or project he was updating us on.

As instructed, we gathered in our dressing room, and were surprised when Sarah Trahern, the CEO of the Country Music Hall of Fame came in. She said, "I'm going to get right to the point. The Oak Ridge Boys have been selected to become members of the Country Music Hall of Fame."

The room was completely silent. We were all speechless. We did not expect it at all. After a moment, we all hugged Jim, and then we hugged Sarah. Then Duane, Joe, Richard and I all hugged each other. We were all in tears.

As we tried to regain our composure, Sarah said, "There is one big catch…You can't tell anyone. It has to be a secret until we make the public announcement in March." She said we could tell our wives, but no one else. And if we did spill the beans and it got out in the public, it would all be off. They would deny we were chosen, and the honor would go to someone else. We all somehow kept the biggest secret of our lives. But it was a long two months!

Grand Ole Opry star Jim Ed Brown and the late musician Grady Martin were both inducted into the Hall the same year that we were. Jim Ed Brown had been battling cancer all that year. While we were all announced as the next Hall of Fame members in March, the official induction ceremony wasn't until October. When Jim Ed's health began to fail, the decision was made to present him with his Hall of Fame medal that June. The ceremony was done in his hospital room, and Jim Ed passed away just a week later.

So many of the people I listened to when I was a little boy are in the Hall of Fame. Their plaques are on the wall of the Hall, but the people themselves are gone now. For us to be given the honor while we were still around, and while we could still cherish it and appreciate it, made it even more special.

On October 25, 2015, The Oak Ridge Boys were inducted into the Country Music Hall of Fame. During the ceremony, Trisha Yearwood and Garth Brooks performed our hit, "I'll Be True to You." Then, our long-time friend Kenny Rogers came out and surprised us as he said, "I am so happy to be the one to induct you into the Hall of Fame."

Joe, Richard, Duane and I took turns saying our "Thank You's," and when my turn came, I ad-libbed, "I know some of you are thinking, 'Well, how the hell did he get in here?' But thank you all. I love you. I wouldn't take nothin' for this moment right now. Thank you very much."

There is a lot of great talent in country music that never made it into the Hall of Fame. If you're in country music, it is the top of the mountain.

SIMONE

I got married for the 4th (and final) time on August 29, 2015.

My bride was a wonderful woman named Simone. We had first met when I was 40 years old…but I was 75 on our wedding day.

I knew that Simone didn't marry me for my money. Because I didn't have any. After you go through 3 divorces, you pretty much lose everything.

When we reconnected in 2009, I told her that she scared me. I knew my weaknesses, but I did not want to jeopardize my family and my son. I was thrilled to death to be Solomon's dad. Simone told me that she respected my family and we both continued to stay close as friends only. No one would believe that nothing physical was going on between Simone and I, but that was the absolute truth.

In 2013, 3 months after I was served divorce papers, I called Simone. Then I called her every night. I looked forward to those talks. I poured my heart out to her, and she was such a calming voice, as I shared all the drama and trauma I was dealing with. We got to know each other on the phone over the course of a few months.

Simone can tell our story better than I can:

"I was a fan of William's before we ever met. When I saw his picture on the cover of their "Together" album, I thought he was so handsome. As I looked at the picture, I knew that I would meet William in person one day. I didn't know how, and I didn't know when, but I knew that I was going to meet this man. I attended my first Oak Ridge Boys concert when I was 18 years old. It was October of 1980 at Great America Theme Park in San Jose, and I was blown away. Girls were fighting to get a scarf from William. I was in the front row, and William saw me and tossed a scarf my way. But before I could catch it, two other women jumped in front of me and got it. A minute later, he took a scarf and held out his hand until I got up and took it. I still have that scarf today, along with two others that he gave me during his concerts.

I didn't get to meet William that night, but I would a short time later, when I went with my friend Karen to see the Oaks at Knotts Berry Farm. We stayed at the same hotel as the group and as William was walking through the lobby, he stopped and we took a photo. So, I have a picture of the moment we first met. Not many couples have a photo of that moment.

When I was 19, I went to see the group in Sparks, Nevada on New Year's Eve. I got to visit with William backstage, but there was a lot of partying going on, and there were so many people around, that it was hard to have a conversation. But I could tell we were making a connection. We started developing a very close, true friendship.

William and I had a couple things in common. We were both very shy and we both loved art. I had been taking oil painting lessons, and in January of 1982, I did a portrait of William. I gave it to him when the Oaks performed at the Cow Palace in San Francisco. I had put the painting in a pillow case to protect it, and when William took it out, his face just lit up. He was so proud of me and was touched that I would give him this special gift.

The next month, I went with him when the Oaks performed at the Houston Astrodome. But after that show, I would not see William again for more than 26 years. I went on with my life and he went on with his. But I often wondered if he still had the painting I had given him.

In 2009, William was on his third marriage and I had been through two. William's mother had died a year earlier, and my mother had just passed away. I was still in a deep state of grief when I agreed to go with my cousin Lisa to see the Oaks at the Alabama Theater in Myrtle Beach. Before the show, as we were walking into our hotel, William was coming out. I walked up and said, 'William, it's Simone. Do you remember me?' More than two and a half decades had passed. He got the biggest smile on his face, and said, 'Good Lord Simone, I could never forget you. I have thought of you many times and I've always wondered if life was good to you.'

I was so thankful and amazed we were able to talk again, even if it was for just a couple minutes. I was excited and so full of joy that we had reconnected. William asked for my phone number and I was overwhelmed to think that he and I were going to become friends again. I asked William if he had saved the portrait I had painted of him more than 25 years earlier. He blew my mind when he answered, "Simone, I kept it all these years. I even pulled it out of the rubble after the tornado wiped out our home." Then he surprised me by saying, "Even though it was a painting of me, every time I looked at it, I saw your face."

William gave me some art magazines and encouraged me to get back into painting. I couldn't believe that someone like him wanted to help me emotionally and would give me such encouragement when I really needed it. I never got that emotional encouragement from any other man.

A few months after his wife filed for divorce, William called me. Over the next few months, our friendship grew into something much more…all over the phone. In the summer of 2013, we finally started seeing each other. William took me to his childhood home in Alabama. I was surprised to learn that we both had similar religious upbringings and backgrounds. We knew a lot of the same gospel groups, like the Rambos. I was a fan of them, and he had worked with them.

During that time, William had to win over my daughter, who was very protective of me. They had a long conversation, and she told him that she was not going to let another man hurt her mother. He admired that, and they have the sweetest relationship now.

In April of 2014, William flew to Amarillo, Texas, loaded me and my pets up in a U-Haul and drove us all to Nashville. It was freezing cold, with snow on the ground, and he literally came to my rescue. He stopped everything he was doing to move me here, all by himself. That's the kind of person he is. I've never had any other person do something like that for me.

Of course, William is a little bit older than me. But I was never concerned about our age difference. It was never an issue. He's in such good shape. He might have white hair, but he acts much younger than many 50-year-old men. I wish William could have met my parents. I don't know if my mother would have accepted him since he was so much older than me and with him being in the entertainment field. But he would have loved to have had the chance to meet her.

William didn't officially propose to me until our wedding rehearsal! We just kind of started making plans to get married. But as we finished our rehearsal, William got me alone and said, 'I have nothing to give you, but myself. All my money is gone. I don't even have a home. I just have me. Will you marry me Simone?' It was so sweet.

We were married in Nashville, and all our family members and lots of friends, including the Oak Ridge Boys were all in attendance. William's long-time friend and lawyer Wayne Halper officiated the ceremony, and Jim Halsey surprised us both by presenting us with an eagle feather, which represents the Native American spiritual blessing of Union and the sacred Circle of love. Our matching wedding bands are each inscribed with the Hebrew words from the Song of Solomon 6:3, "I am my beloved's, and my beloved is mine."

After our wedding, we returned to our little home in Burns, Tennessee. The Oaks were heading out to a concert the following day, so we never had an actual honeymoon. But the night of our wedding, as we danced outside, in the grass, William took a photo of the moon. We laughed as he said, "This is our honeymoon in the sky."

During the first year of our marriage, we lived in that little house in the middle of nowhere. It was a great time that I will treasure. We both loved living there, but then, William was able to get his former home back. I was a little leery at first, since it was a place he had shared with his ex-wife. But when I saw his routine with all the animals, the deer, turkeys and other wildlife on our property, I knew it was where he needed to be. This land and William go hand in hand, and we made it into our home.

One of the things we have in common is the hurt we share when our children have to leave us. My daughter Megan and granddaughter Matilda live in Tulsa, Oklahoma, and when they come to visit and then have to leave, I get into such a funk. It hurts so much. And that's the way William is with Solomon. When Solomon has to go home, it breaks William's heart. When your kids don't live close, it's horrible when they have to leave. But I'm sure that every parent and grandparent reading this can also relate to that.

The year 2020, with the pandemic, was scary at times, not only for us, but for everyone. We spent the first two months of the lockdown, totally by ourselves. We didn't leave the house. After William had been deathly ill earlier in the year, we didn't want to risk going out, so we had our groceries delivered to our porch. I was very concerned about him catching the virus, and we didn't have visitors for a couple months.

Watching the concert dates fall like dominos and watching our finances go down, was also scary. But the lockdown gave us the opportunity of being together that we never had before. We were able to spend quality time with each other and we plan to continue that. When the Oaks crank back up and hit the road for 200 dates a year again, we will continue to make our time together more about the quality than the quantity.

I was a fan of the Oak Ridge Boys before I ever met William, and I still have the same excitement when I go to an Oaks show today, as I did when I was 18 years old. I love their music, and it brings back so many memories when I listen to them. The group has such a catalogue, that there's no way they can sing all their hits in one show. And William's voice is stronger today than it ever was, and when I listen to him, I am in awe.

People ask me what is the best part about being married to William, and it's hard to put that into words. But he is just so loving. He is respectful. He has such a love and respect that I have never experienced before. I love him so much.

I keep a little journal of what I call "William-isms." When he says something profound or funny, I will write it down. There seem to be a lot more funny things than profound! Here are a few he has said in recent months:

"My swagger has become a stagger."

"I am a has-been that never was."

"Some people don't understand my lack of humor."

"My meditation is sitting around, thinking about shit."

People also ask me, 'What is William really like?' Here are a few things that you might not know:

William is quite shy. He doesn't say much in public, but once he starts talking, he doesn't stop. But in public or a group setting, he's very quiet. He likes for people to think he's dumb, but he is taking everything in. When he's sitting there, not saying anything, he's hearing every word that everyone else is saying, and he doesn't forget anything.

He had never worn flip-flops before he met me. We would be in Florida and he'd have boots on. I wanted him to loosen up and have fun and not be so serious. He is much more relaxed today than he used to be.

I've never seen anyone laugh as hard as he does. When he gets tickled about something, I start laughing because he is laughing so hard. And his laugh becomes louder and harder. We laugh at ourselves all the time. William is a funny guy, and I didn't realize what a sense of humor he has. He has a way with words, and he can do and say things that have me doubled over, laughing. It is refreshing to see that side of him, and I wish his fans and everyone else had the chance to see that side, but I think he saves it for those he is very close with.

People say he lived in a teepee. He never did. He had a teepee on his property, outside his house. He spent lots of time in the teepee, but he didn't live there.

Ice cream makes William cough. That also happened to his mother when she ate ice cream.

His favorite saying…at least to me is, 'Simmer down.'

And before he says that again, I will close with this: When I found out he was going to write a book, I thought "Uh-Oh. Oh boy." I probably said that because I know he is not afraid to tell the truth. He is genuine and honest, almost to a fault. He can be almost too honest. But I was thrilled when he told me he was writing his life story. I can't wait to read some of the stories. I know there are things that I still don't know about him."

– Simone

As I was working on this book, Simone and I spent our 5th anniversary at the Kentucky State Fair. That might not be the most exotic place to celebrate, but it was kind of appropriate for us. The Oaks were scheduled to sing the National Anthem at the fair, so Simone rode on the bus and we had a steak dinner with the whole group. I was thankful that at least we could be together.

Simone keeps me grounded, and she knows all the struggles I have been through over the years. She is devoted to her daughter Megan and granddaughter Matilda, and they are wonderful.

I am so thankful to have Simone to share this season of my life. She is someone I can lean on. She has been there to support me mentally, physically, spiritually, and emotionally.

In 2020, when the pandemic hit, one blessing to the lockdowns was that I was able to be sheltered at home with Simone. Because of the Oaks' constant touring, she and I had never had time to be together for very long. Usually when the group has a couple days off, those are always spent running errands and getting ready to go back out.

During the first two months of our downtime, Simone fixed the most incredible meals, with desserts and all the trimmings. Every day was another new gourmet meal, and she made amazing cakes, pies and pudding.

That went on for two and a half months. Then it came to an abrupt end. Simone said, "I'm gaining too much weight and I am not going to cook anymore big meals." I still enjoy every minute we get to spend together…but I miss all that great food!

MAKING AMENDS

> "Forgiveness is as healing for us as it is for the one we forgive."
>
> – Charlie Daniels

I've admitted to many mistakes in my life. Telling the truth, good or bad, has always come easily for me. But asking for forgiveness for my mistakes has not been as easy.

For a number of years, my wife Simone encouraged me to apologize to my first wife Frogene for my unfaithfulness during our marriage. I was proud of Simone, that she would be so concerned about my ex-wife. Not many wives would be that way. But she cared about Frogene, and she cared about me, and she wanted things to be right between us all.

While I knew Simone was right, I didn't go immediately to Frogene. I kept putting it off as weeks turned into months, and months turned into years. About once a month, Simone would ask, 'Have you called her yet?' My answer was always 'No.' Simone asked, 'What are you waiting on?' I promised her I would, but I kept putting it off. Until Thanksgiving Day, 2018.

My son Chris invited Simone and me over to spend Thanksgiving at his house. He told us his girlfriend, my son Craig and Frogene would all be there. Frogene was always a great cook and she helped prepare a wonderful meal. Everyone had a beautiful day of fellowship.

After dessert, as everyone else was starting to gather the dishes, I went to Frogene and said, "I want to apologize to you Frogene. You didn't deserve to have an unfaithful husband. I am so sorry for all the crap I put you through." I spoke from my heart, and I put everything out there, adding "Every problem we ever had was my fault. I just hope you will be able to forgive me."

I was crying, and through my tears, I could see she was also crying. But through her tears, she smiled the biggest smile and said, "William, I forgave you years ago."

I looked around the room and everyone was in tears. We were all crying. It was a very emotional day. I looked at Simone and she was kind of shaking her head in disbelief. Here are her thoughts and also those from my son Craig about that day:

> "That day was an out-of-body experience. I couldn't believe it was happening. For years, I had been on William to make things right with Frogene. I could see the love that Rusty, Chris and Craig had for both their parents, and I know it was very hard on them when they divorced. But I always thought William would apologize in private, with just the two of them. I had no idea he would do it with me there and everyone else also in the room! When he started talking, I immediately started sweating bullets. I was about to die. I thought, 'William, you are not going to do this right here.' But he sure did.
>
> I didn't know how Frogene was going to receive it. But it couldn't have gone any better or been any more perfect. It was so sweet, and it was like a 1,000 pound weight was lifted off William and also off Frogene. It was one memorable Thanksgiving. I was so glad he did it."
>
> — Simone

> "Thanksgiving, 2018 was a great day. It was an emotional day. We were all choked up. It is not easy to

> apologize for your mistakes, especially in front of a house full of your family members. But it was something that needed to be done, and the timing was perfect."
>
> — Craig Golden

I thought that Thanksgiving, with all my family there, was the perfect setting for me to bare my soul. The thing that made it even more special was that I did it when I WANTED to, and didn't wait until I HAD to. If I had waited a few more months, it would have felt more like I was obligated to say I was sorry.

Everyone was healthy and happy on that Thanksgiving Day, 2018. But one year later, when we all got together again, Frogene was fighting for her life. She had been diagnosed with a fatal cancer.

2020 was a horrible year for many people. It was devastating for most musicians and artists. But for me and my family, it allowed us to be there for Frogene. My sons got to spend the entire year with her, and with the Oaks tour dates all cancelled, I was also able to visit with her throughout the year.

As she fought her cancer, I watched my sons honor their mother when she needed it the most. She always had one, two or all three sons with her over her last year. They helped her so much and I was proud to see what responsible sons they were. It was a God gift that they were able to spend so much time with their mother. It was a bright side to the year of pandemic shutdowns. Chris' girlfriend Marie was a wonderful caretaker for Frogene and they became very close during that time. My son Rusty adds these thoughts:

> "My parents' relationship during their last couple years...what a blessing. It's sad that it took something like that to bring the family so close, but God works in mysterious ways. I knew that mom always loved him. And even though he went through a few wives, I knew he loved her too."   — Rusty Golden

Frogene passed away on July 2, 2020. As I prepared to go to the funeral in Brewton, Duane Allen called and said he had arranged to take our tour bus there. Duane and his wife Norah Lee had always been such wonderful friends to Frogene. They loved her and all our Golden family. Duane paid for the bus, the driver and fuel and we all went to Alabama together. Ronnie Fairchild and his wife Kim also rode with us.

As soon as the service at the gravesite was over, I walked over and got in Craig's car. I had left my phone in the car, and the moment I opened it, I had a text message that said, "RIP Charlie Daniels." I couldn't believe it. I was still in the cemetery after burying my first wife and that was the first thing I saw. It was one bad day. I sat there and thought, 'I am in the valley of the shadow of death…but I will fear no evil, because I know He is with us.'

A 20-20 VISION

2020 was a year of sickness for millions of people. I started the year quite healthy, but a short time after I celebrated my 81st birthday, I was so sick that I couldn't get out of bed.

The Oak Ridge Boys kicked off 2020 with a full schedule. We spent the last week of January performing on a country music cruise to St. Maarten and San Juan. As always, the ship was full of lots of people from other countries, including many of the ship's employees. When the cruise was over, we flew straight to Las Vegas, where we caught our bus to a week of concerts in Laughlin, Nevada.

We performed 11 shows in 7 days in Laughlin. The day of our last show there, I started feeling terrible. But I got through the concert and we rode the bus back to Las Vegas, where we caught a plane back home to Nashville. We had just one day off, before we had to fly to New York City to appear on a number of network TV shows. I spent my entire off day between Nevada and New York in bed. I was too weak to even sit up.

But when the plane flew to the Big Apple the next morning, I was on it. I made the trip to New York, but my condition continued to get worse with each passing hour. My legs and body were aching. My bones were hurting so bad. I had never had that feeling. I looked forward to getting back home, but I knew our heavy schedule was not over yet. The night after we returned to Tennessee, we were scheduled to play the Grand Ole Opry. I stayed in bed right up until showtime at the Opry. I was having chills and fever, but I somehow managed to make it on stage.

The next day, I went to the doctor. By then, I was coughing. The doctor said I had bronchitis and they gave me a Z-pack. A week later I was having even more trouble. The doctor gave me heavy anti-biotics, and I took those every 12 hours for the next 4 days. But nothing seemed to help. I was lying in bed and my leg bones hurt like never before. I knew something was very wrong with me.

I was in bed for two weeks, before I finally wound up at the medical place up the road from me. They pulled my blood, ran tests, and found that my sodium level was at a dangerously low level. They put me in an ambulance and took me to Vanderbilt hospital. For the next 3 days, I was in the Intensive Care Unit with Influenza B. The doctors gradually brought my sodium up, and I started slowly coming back around.

While I was in the hospital and then as I recovered at home, the Oaks still had concerts to do. So, they brought in my friend Michael Sykes to fill in for me for a couple weeks. He didn't have time to rehearse, but he had studied us so much over the years, that he knew each guy's part, and he did a great job. When I told him about my book, Michael said he wanted to say a few words about his time as an Oak Ridge Boy:

> "After being such a fan of the Oaks when I was a little boy, all these years later, to be up on stage singing with them was a surreal moment. I was so honored to be up there with my heroes, and it was an awesome feeling to be with them. But at the same time, as I looked out at the crowd, I was thinking to myself, 'I know there are some real disappointed people out there, because William isn't here.'

I knew the people in that audience were expecting a tall guy with a long beard to walk out here. Here I am…short, with no beard. As we got ready to go on stage, I told Richard, 'This is a sobering position to be in.'

I had already told the Boys that I didn't want to sing any of the songs that William sang lead on, and there was no way I would even attempt to perform 'Thank God for Kids.' I didn't want that crowd to turn on me!

I could never fill William's shoes, but I sure had fun trying them on for a couple weeks. A few months later, William asked me to help produce a few songs he was going to do with his sons. Those 'few songs' turned out to be 3 different albums! It also turned out to be one of the best things I've ever been involved with. When people ask me, 'What is it like to work with William Lee Golden?' I tell them, 'If you were an actor, how would it feel to meet and work with John Wayne? That's how it is for me when I met and got to work with William Lee Golden."

— Michael Sykes

When you're performing live every night for 50 years, there are bound to be some nights when you don't feel like singing all night. It's on those nights that you need to dig down deep. Entertaining is like any other job. If you're not feeling good, you still have to go in, and do the best you can. We've all sung with fevers and when we were under the weather. But we are fortunate, because if one of us is sick or having a bad night, we know the other 3 guys are there to step up and cover for us. And if one of us is having something serious going on, we have band members who can step in temporarily to make sure we don't have to cancel a date.

The whole band and crew depends on those concert dates. Our big money comes from concert performances, but the show must go on, in order for everyone to get paid. I appreciated Michael Sykes covering for me. He helped save the show and they didn't have to cancel the concerts. It's a good thing they did the shows while I was sick, because just a few months later, almost every show for the rest of the year was cancelled due to the virus lockdowns.

While I was told that I had the flu, a month after I got out of the hospital, we started hearing about the first cases of the Corona virus starting to hit the U.S. But I feel like I might have had it before anyone knew what it was. Thankfully, once I got over my illness, I enjoyed great health throughout 2020. I needed to be in good health…because I was about to embark on one of the most ambitious years of my life.

As I write this, I am now 82 years old. I was 25 when I joined the Oak Ridge Boys.

I think the word "Boys" in our name, helps keep us young…at least in our minds. I have tried my best to also stay young in body. Today, I am in better shape than many 55-year-olds.

My daddy always told me, "You've got to keep yourself in shape. A man never gets too old to build muscle. If you treat yourself like an invalid, you will become an invalid. You have to move and be active." While I've never joined a gym, I love to exercise, but most of that comes when I'm outside, doing work around my property.

Every week or so, I go to Tractor Supply and buy a dozen 40 to 50 pound bags of bird seed and deer corn. I can still throw those heavy bags in and out of my vehicle. I feed the birds, deer and squirrels each morning, and I don't allow myself to sit under my shade tree to enjoy watching the wildlife until all my chores are done.

To keep myself in shape, I try to walk every day. That builds up my wind, gets my legs strong, and makes me feel younger. I try to walk 10, 000 steps a day on very hot days, when its over 90 degrees. In past years, I would walk at least 6 miles a day, and many days, I'd go 12 miles. That included days when we were on tour. As soon as our bus arrives in a town, I usually get out and start walking. Since I'm now in my 80s, I've cut back a little, and only walk about 4 miles each day. But I still walk as much as I can, and I feel bad if I don't walk every day.

I also do sit ups. I try to do a total of 150 a day, 25 at a time. I'll do 25, then catch my breath, and then do another 25. I can do 6 reps of 25 in about 20 minutes. I like to do those in my hotel room on the afternoon before our concert. It gives me more energy and really helps my breathing and singing.

One of my doctors told me that he had seen many thin 95-year-old men. But he had never seen a fat 95-year-old man. So that kind of motivated me to keep my weight down. I try to get my rest, eat healthy and stay active. I'm also thankful that I have great vision. I don't use glasses and I can see the deer and turkey 100 yards across my yard.

When the pandemic lockdown hit in the Spring of 2020, like millions of other people, I found myself with a lot of time on my hands, and I thought it would be a great time to try to get my life story down on paper. So, I started writing this book. I sometimes shook my head as I thought, "Of all people, for me to be a writer…I don't have the vocabulary to be a writer. I'm the guy who never talks on stage." But my co-writer, Scot England assured me, "Your fans want it in your own words. Be yourself and just tell your story, and they will love it." Ironically, as I looked back at my life, I started looking ahead, and I became very excited about my future.

This book made me want to revisit who I am musically. Rather than sitting around, watching all the negative stuff on TV, and worrying if we'd ever do another show this year, I headed outside…with a song in my heart, and songs in my head. As I walked my property, I was actually going back to where I came from. I started hearing all the old gospel songs I was raised on when I was little. Songs started coming to me, and I couldn't get them out of my mind.

I sing gospel songs all day. They come to my mind and I sing them as I drive, or as I feed the deer and squirrels around my home. I spent most of the lockdown singing classic gospel songs, just for myself, around the house. I still love that music and it kept me in good voice during our downtime.

If you stopped by my house in 2020, you would have found me, either singing, or just sitting in total quiet. I grew up in a quiet place, way out in the country and I have always loved being quiet, and I still need to have quiet time. It helps keep me calm and gives me time to sort everything out in my mind.

During the uncertain times we've been living in over the last year or two, I found my blood pressure rising as I watched all the bad news on TV. I decided that I shouldn't stress myself out over things that I have no control over. I needed to step away from the hate and negative energy, so I turned off the television and sat in quiet. I wanted to allow my mind to think about positive and creative things.

In an effort to get total peace and quiet, I went back to our family farm in Alabama. Being on the farm where I grew up always helped stimulate my imagination. During that time, I reflected back on my life, remembered stories from my past, and in my quiet moments, I saw a clear vision of my future:

I saw myself making a new album with my sons, and we would be singing those old gospel songs that had been going through my head.

I booked the studio time and hired some of the best musicians in Nashville. I also asked Ben Isaacs and Michael Sykes to be our producers for the project. My initial plan was to go in and do 3 to 6 songs with Chris and Rusty. But when we heard how great the songs sounded, we decided to do more. We could feel we were doing something very special, because the music was moving everyone who heard it. Over the course of a few months, we recorded 33 songs! We did enough for a gospel album and then we did a CD of the country songs that I was raised on.

In addition to getting all the audio recorded, I also hired a professional video crew to film every minute of us in the studio. To make sure that it was done right, I asked my best friend Jeff Panzer to come out of retirement to supervise all the video production. I also asked Jeff to give his thoughts on that for this book:

"In the middle of a pandemic, my phone rang and it was William. He said, 'Panzer, I'm going into the studio tomorrow. I hired a video crew to shoot everything, and I was wondering if you could get on a plane tonight and come to Nashville to oversee everything.'

I said, 'William, you have to be kidding. I'm not getting on an airplane in the middle of this pandemic. My whole city and state are closed down. I'm over 60 with pre-existing conditions, and I'm not flying to Nashville.'

But I called the head of the television crew and we talked things over. We arranged that I would produce and direct the entire recording session from my home in California. We did it all through our I-phones! I was able to see everything they were filming, and I could direct them and tell them the different shots I wanted.

As I watched the live feed, I couldn't believe what I was seeing. I saw an 81-year-old man sing like I've never heard him sing before. He nailed it. I've always believed in William and in his creativity, but all this new music was really amazing. It was exciting to watch.

He was making the greatest music of his life, with no record label support. It was a huge task. He was footing the entire bill himself, and he had assembled the team of players and producers he wanted. William wanted to show the true talents Rusty and Chris have. I think that being the sons of William was kind of a blessing and a curse to both Chris and Rusty, but this really shows how great they are.

One of the many highlights on the project came when William asked his son Craig to sing two songs. William had a vision and an idea of getting Craig in the studio. Craig had always been very shy, but he always told me, 'I think I can sing better than these guys.' I thought he was kidding, until I finally heard him sing this year. I was blown away as Chris, Rusty, Craig and William turned into their own quartet. I couldn't believe how great Craig sang. I asked him, 'Where have you been hiding for the last 30 years?'

Over the last 40 years, I've watched William when he focuses in on something, and has something he wants to accomplish. He goes for it with everything he has, and he does everything he needs to do to reach his goals. When someone has a spark like that, you want to go with it. You want to be on the train with him, because you know he is going to take you to some amazing places.

Most 81 and 82-year-olds are thinking about what nursing home they were going to go to. But William is so driven and so focused on writing his book, and recording his new music, and he just never stops. After all these years of knowing him, he is still inspiring me."

— Jeff Panzer

Thanks to Jeff's video expertise, our recording sessions will be the foundation of at least one, and possibly a couple television specials. The farther we got into our project, the more excited I got about everything. The more pumped up I got, the grander my plans became, and of course the more expensive everything became. When you think big, it costs big.

But I was more than willing to pay whatever it took in order to make my dream come true. I've never liked asking other people to put up money for my ideas. I always try to save up my own money in advance, so I'll be ready when something comes up. But I don't have money to waste or lose.

Such an undertaking is a pretty big risk and gamble. But there are times in life, when you need to take a risk. The people who go out on a limb and aren't afraid to take risks are the people who do great things. I can be in Las Vegas for two weeks, and I'll not even look at a slot machine. I won't gamble one nickel. But when it comes to a musical project, something I feel passionate about and something that I feel I know something about, I will take that gamble every day. I gambled on the Oak Ridge Boys when everyone else said they would never happen, and of course it paid off.

I started this huge project during the time when all our income had stopped, since all the Oaks' concerts were cancelled because of the pandemic. But instead of trying to hold on to the money we had in the bank, I was spending money on studio musicians and film crews. My wife Simone probably didn't appreciate seeing our savings account falling, but she had faith in me. She knew that I was betting on myself. I believed in myself, and she also believed in me.

This was a major project that I wanted to create. But you've got to be able to see it in your mind before you can get it into the studio. My son Chris helped keep all the sessions running smoothly. Here are some of his thoughts on the new music we've been making:

> "The best part of this entire project is watching Dad as he listens to the playback in the studio. You can see the joy on his face and the pride in his heart as he listens to

the song we just recorded. When he hears it in the speakers for the first time, his reaction is just priceless.

He had asked me and Rusty to be a part of the sessions, but then he wanted our entire family to be involved. My kids sang and played on it. Elijah sang a couple songs, Elizabeth played fiddle and Elizabeth and Rebekah both sang background vocals on a song or two. I swelled with pride watching my kids in the studio. I love watching them get to show their talents. Dad always put everyone else up front. He has done that his entire career. He always liked to give other people the chance to shine.

One of the highlights of my career was the night of November 23, 2015. I was playing with Restless Heart at the Christmas 4 Kids concert at the Ryman Auditorium in Nashville. They asked me to sing 'Thank God for Kids.' Through some miracle, the Oaks were in Nashville that night, so dad drove downtown to see me. He was by himself and he was very under the weather. He was really sick. I sang half the song, and then Dad walked out on stage, unannounced, and he sang the second half. The place just went crazy. They gave us a standing ovation that went on and on. Afterward, he said, 'This was good medicine for me.' I said, 'Well, it was a highlight of my life.'

Dad's plan is to sing with the Oak Ridge Boys until they retire, and then he will hit the road with us, and we will perform as The Goldens until he's 101. To anyone else, that would sound impossible. But not to William Lee Golden. I think the biggest challenge is, the rest of us are gonna have to get in shape, so we can hang with Dad over the next 20 years. There is only one William Lee Golden. I am so proud of him and I'm so proud he's my dad."

— Chris Golden

As we recorded day after day, I was so proud as I watched Chris and Rusty. They were going through so many bad things outside the studio. They had just lost their mother and their careers had been shut down because of the virus. But they blocked all that out and made the greatest music they've ever made. Chris and Rusty are multi-talented and it shows on this. It shows what power players they are capable of being. As a father, it makes my heart swell with joy and I also want people to see what wonderful men they are.

Back when they were making records as The Goldens, Chris and Rusty were both very good. But they are both so much better today. Over the last couple of decades, they've matured as men and as musicians, as they've played with the best players in the country. Chris is incredible, and he put so much effort into all of this. Rusty also really stepped up and he understands how to make great records. They both can do solo shows just by themselves. Chris does concerts with just his guitar and piano, and Rusty has done that overseas, in other countries, just him and his piano. Rusty's vocals have gotten so strong since he's been performing by himself. I was very impressed when I heard him a couple years ago, and we all started singing together again in the spring of 2020.

My sons are solid men who I can depend on. They're great musicians and real professionals. We have a mutual respect for each other. When Chris, Rusty and I were touring the country together in late '80s and '90s, my son Craig drove our bus. But I always knew that Craig was a great singer. He was too shy and timid to pursue it, and I think when he saw how talented his brothers were, maybe he felt he couldn't compete with them. But when he sang around the house, he always had a great voice, so I asked him to do a couple southern rock songs on our new project. Here are his thoughts:

> "I was always an outdoor kid. I loved being outside all the time. I loved hunting and trapping and fishing. My

brothers were inside, playing music and I was always outside. They were great at music when they were young. When Chris and Rusty were performing as The Goldens, I was driving their tour bus. It was my first driving gig. I helped them load the gear and equipment and sold their merchandise.

When they were having their biggest success, I had just gotten married and was a new father. My father-in-law was in construction and he taught me how to build houses. Dad told me, 'I can't draw a picture of a house and you are building them.' But on the weekends, I would drive the bus for The Goldens.

2020 was a devastating year financially for all of us. Every one of my bus driving jobs was cancelled because there were no concerts. But that turned into a huge blessing that allowed me to be there when my mother was dying. Any other year, I would have never had the time to be with her. It also gave us all the time to be a part of my dad's new music projects.

I waited a long time to start singing in public. I would drive the buses for the artists and I'd think, I should be pursuing my dream of singing. I didn't want to live with the regret of never trying to reach my goal, and I'm thankful that my dad pushed me to finally step out into the spotlight a little bit. I was so scared, and it was exactly as Dad had described it to me. He said, 'It is like getting naked in front of everyone.' You have to put yourself out there, but there's nothing better than being in the studio with my brothers and my dad."

– Craig Golden

With my sons and grandchildren all taking part, the new music turned into a true family affair. I've always wondered if any of my grandkids would follow in my footsteps. Chris' son

Elijah is writing songs, singing and recording, and all my grandkids are musically talented.

On the new project, I sing lead on most of the songs, while Rusty sings baritone right under me. Chris sings in the upper part of his range and Aaron McCune sings bass. Aaron is known for his work with Dailey and Vincent, and he helped give our songs a magical sound.

Steve Hinson played the dobro, and as I was planning everything, Steve was the one I wanted all along. Every musician played so great, and the sound is as good, and maybe even better than I had imagined.

Ben Issacs was blown away with our sound. Ben told me that my performance on "Too Much to Gain to Lose," the old Dottie Rambo song, was the greatest vocal performance that he had ever been a part of. I couldn't believe it. He has produced so many amazing singers, including the Oak Ridge Boys, so his compliment was high praise.

I had lots of time to devote to my Golden family music project, as the pandemic lockdowns canceled 100 Oak Ridge Boys concerts in 2020. In the history of the group, they had never had as much time off. For me, it was a blessing to have so much uninterrupted time at home with my wife. I'm sure Duane, Richard and Joe all felt the same way.

The time off during 2020 was a godsend to me. It gave us a chance to work on other projects, and more importantly, it allowed us to recharge our batteries and get back in shape, so we will be ready to work even harder once the world returns to normal.

As we watched the concert dates fall off our calendar, there was one date that we kept an especially close eye on. It was our concert at the Kentucky State Fair. We were booked to perform at the fair for the 45th straight year. Yes, every single year, for the past four and a half decades, every August, you knew you would see the Oak Ridge Boys at the Kentucky State Fair.

There is no other act in any form of music that has played one fair every year for that many years in a row. But when the State Fair was cancelled due to Covid, it looked like our record streak would come to an end. But at the last minute, Jim Halsey emailed us and said that we would be heading to Kentucky.

While the fair wasn't going to be open to fans or the public, it would allow participants to compete in different events and the World's Championship Horse Show would also continue. We didn't get to do our entire concert, but we did keep our 45-year performance streak intact, as we sang the National Anthem before the Championship Horse Show.

It was an odd feeling to sing in front of an almost empty Kentucky Exposition Center. But it was even weirder when we performed to a totally empty Grand Ole Opry House. For a number of months, even though no one could attend the Opry, the show did go on. While it seemed eerie to sing with no audience, we still gave everything we had to our performance. We knew that millions of people were tuned in to watch the Opry on TV, and they were also listening to us on WSM radio.

As 2020 turned to 2021, and as I celebrated my 82nd birthday, I felt a desperation to get this book and the new recordings with my sons finished. That urgency grew as I said goodbye to so many close friends who died in 2020. Those included Kenny Rogers, Charlie Daniels, Harold Reid of the Statler Brothers, and Jimmy Capps, who played on almost all our hits.

As I read each of their obituaries, I was struck by the fact that most of those men were my exact age when they died. Recently, I've also lost a lot of friends who are younger than me, and that's sobering to think about.

Gary McSpadden, the man I always called the "Coolest Oak Ridge Boy" during their gospel years also died in 2020. That same year, we also lost Skip Mitchell and a few years earlier, Don Breland passed away. Skip and Don had played in the Oaks band and also toured with The Goldens in the 1980s and '90s. Mark Ellerbee, who was the Oaks' drummer for more than a decade, died in 2013. With those amazing people gone, I realize that I'm lucky to still be here. I need to make the most of the time I have left, and I refuse to waste one day.

THE FUTURE

I am always dreaming. I will never stop dreaming until my last breath.

I have been out there singing for a long time. But it doesn't seem as long as it has been. When you get this far into your career, you realize how lucky you are to still have a career. But then I realize how much there is that I haven't done, and I would still like to do, before it's too late.

My dad worked hard all his life. He worked right up to the end, when he died at the age of 75. As I write this, I'm 7 years older than dad was when he left this earth. I feel like every day is a gift, and I make sure to never take any day for granted. Daddy used to say, "Life is short. If a man lives to be 100, it still ain't very long on this earth." My mom used to tell me, "The older you get, the faster that times goes by." They were both right. When I hit 75, the next 5 years just seemed to fly by.

In 1987, our manager, Jim Halsey told a reporter, "I can see the Oak Ridge Boys still making music 40 years from now." I'm sure some people laughed at that crazy prediction. But now, more than 44 years later, we are not only still here, but we are making some of the greatest music we've ever made. It takes experience to get good at your craft, and after you do 200 shows a year for 4 or 5 decades, you should be pretty good at what you do.

The Oak Ridge Boys are all still here, and so are our fans. We still sell out most of our shows, as people come see us sing all our hits. And now those songs take the fans back to the time when they first heard us. Our audiences today have such a wide range of ages. The older men and women who were there for our first country hits, have brought their children to our shows. And now those kids are grown up and are bringing their own children to see us.

I remember a funny conversation my son Chris had with Richard Sterban as we headed to the bus after a concert. Richard said, "We were here in 1979 and all these beautiful women were out in the audience, wearing short shorts." Chris said, "Richard, these are the same women! They've all gotten older, just like we have."

40 years ago, my brother Ron used to tell me, "People aren't going to keep coming to your shows when you're 70-year-old men." How wrong he was! Now we are 80-year-old men, and people are still packing the house everywhere they play.

Retire? No, there will be no retirement for me. If I had kept my job at the Brewton papermill, I would have been retired years ago. All the guys I went to school with, who are still around, all retired 15 and 20 years ago. And I am still working, out on the road 150 days a year, trying to make a living.

You see very few professional football or basketball players who are over the age of 40. They are usually long retired by then. I'm more than double their age and I'm still working hard! Of course, I love what I do, but I've still got lots of bills to pay. If you go through 3 divorces, and get wiped out financially 3 times, you'll find yourself working into your 80s too.

But will the day come that the Oak Ridge Boys finally park the tour bus for the last time? I'm sure it will. But for now, the bus still has a full gas tank…and so do we. We will continue as long as each guy can go. I think the pause of 2020 possibly extended the group, as we got a well-deserved breather.

I can honestly say that we have never discussed what would happen if one of us couldn't go on. I plan to perform as long as I can, but if I couldn't perform, I would hope the group would go on without me, and I would expect them to. The Oak Ridge Boys were going before any of us were here, and I would certainly never want to be the one who would break up the group.

2021 is the 40th anniversary of "Elvira," so we are doing an "Elvira 40 Tour" all year. Beginning in 2022, we will probably begin a "Farewell Tour." And I hope that we make it a very long farewell, maybe a couple years. But no matter when we take our final encore, I know that we will be giving it all we've got, and we will go out on top.

It's been an interesting ride, and thank God, we are still riding. I've shared my side of the story through this entire book. But before I close, I wanted to give my partners one last chance to have their say:

> "I have never had a closer friend than William Lee. He would do anything for me that he could. He has always been there for me and all of us.
>
> One time, I drove my big tractor into a ditch and got it stuck. The Oak Ridge Boys were having a meeting in their office and William said, 'Let's all go get Duane's tractor out of the ditch.' I told him it was too big for us to push or pull out by hand, but he was willing to go try. When your tractor is stuck in a ditch, you find out who your friends are.
>
> During our shutdown with the Covid virus, we had just 7 shows in 7 months. That was barely enough to pay our utilities. As a group, we said, 'We are not going to be able to have a salary.' William told me, 'Duane, whatever you

feel the Oaks need to do, I am there.' We went through seven months without a full paycheck. William Lee is always on board with all our decisions.

The Oak Ridge Boys will have to retire sometime. But we don't plan on slowing down, at least for the next few years. As long as God grants us with good health, we'll be out there, burning up the road. And when we finally retire, we will retire on top, with our fans still out there screaming, 'Sing Elvira!' and 'Sing Thank God for Kids!' I think one of the most magical moments in country music history is when William sings 'Thank God for Kids.'

I know William has a lot of stories he wants to tell in this book, and I support him 100 percent. He has a lot of fans who want to read about the interesting life he has led.

My friendship and working relationship with William Lee has never been on more solid footing than it is today. We never have a cross word or a disagreement. We are all grandparents and some are great grandparents. We have matured together and aged together, and we're having the best time of our lives right now."

— Duane Allen

"I am honored to be a part of William's book, and I look forward to reading it. Imagine that…I'm with the guy almost every day of the year, and I'm still looking forward to finding out things that I don't know about the man.

I stand right next to William on stage, and I get to see up close, night in and night out, exactly what he does, and it is amazing. I don't know if I've ever been around another person who has the ability that he has to take the lyric of a song and interpret that lyric and communicate it to an audience like he does. He can communicate with the audience better than anyone I have ever seen.

A highlight of our show for many years is when he sings 'Thank God for Kids.' You can tell that he is touching and moving people in the audience as he sings that song. I look out in the audience and the crowd completely changes as he sings it. Couples hold hands and parents or grandparents hug their kids. You always see tears in people's eyes. It is an emotional thing to watch.

Of course, William is the most recognizable member of the group. We can walk through an airport and people spot him before they ever notice the rest of us. If you ever saw me and William Lee walking down the street, you would never think that we have anything in common. But we do, and the main thing we have in common is the love for what we do.

I am honored and thankful that I have had five decades with William. All the Oak Ridge Boys, Joe, Duane, William and myself, we don't see our career as 'work.' We look at it as a labor of love. It is what we love doing and the good Lord above has blessed us with the good health to be able to do it a long time, and I think we still have more songs to sing.

As you've probably already learned in this book, William is a dreamer. He dreams things that are way out there, that the rest of us can't even fathom. His dream for the future and where he wanted to take our group is how I will always remember William. During the years, when they couldn't get booked as a gospel act, William envisioned that the Oak Ridge Boys were going to be a household name one day. He saw that happening…years before it became a reality.

William is the most amazing 82-year-old man in the world. He has an unending supply of energy and he is an inspiration to all of us. I'm a few years younger than him and he certainly sets an example to me. In the latter part of our career, he hasn't let up at all.

It has been an honor to stand next to William on stage…and off, all these years. I don't think I could have chosen a better person to stand next to for almost 50 years."

— Richard Sterban

"In late January of 2021, we did a photo session for our new album, and we did it at Golden's house. We hadn't seen each other in about a month, and when William hugged my neck and said, 'I'm just so glad to have you in my home Joey,' it meant the world to me.

When I was a young singer, before I joined the Oaks, William's advice and constant leadership was something I leaned on. I was basically starving to death when I was with the Keystones, and Golden always told me that I had something special.

William was constantly discussing the importance of dreaming, and he assured me that if I stayed the course and never gave up, I would eventually live out my dreams. He was totally right. Then he helped my dreams come true. It was Golden who called me and offered me the job with the Oak Ridge Boys.

Golden is known for his beard, but his heart is much bigger than his beard. He has such a huge heart. As we have spent our lives together, and as our accomplishments grew, so did our friendship. William's steady friendship and his constant willingness to encourage me and keep

> me positive, has been something I will never be able to repay.
>
> I love William with all my heart. If he needs me, I will be at his side in a heartbeat. I'd stand in front of him and take a bullet. That's how much I love William Lee Golden."
>
> — Joe Bonsall

I thank Joe, Richard and Duane for being a part of my book. But more importantly, I thank them for being a part of my life. They helped my dreams come true, and I'm grateful that I had a role in helping them reach their own dreams. I love, admire, and respect each of those men. For the rest of our lives, if they ever need anything, I will be there for them.

The Oaks have sold over 41 million albums, and we've had the privilege of singing in front of tens of millions of fans. We have been so blessed. But even with our gold and platinum records and every kind of award, I am still not all that impressed with myself. That's why it took me so long to be talked into doing this book. Today, when someone asks me to describe myself, I say, "I'm just a farm boy. I'm a dumb country boy." You hear jokes about ol' country boys. I am that guy. I'm the country boy who rode into town on a collard truck.

Don't get me wrong, I am very proud of all we have accomplished. But some days, I look in the mirror and say, "I'm the has-been that never was." That's the way I see myself.

Over the years, I wanted to see all our dreams come true, and I think most of those have. I wanted the Oaks to not only survive, but to also have longevity, and thank God we did. We all still enjoy being the Oak Ridge Boys, and we look forward to showtime every night. We enjoy traveling to each concert. I love traveling this beautiful country. I've been to some wonderful countries, but none of them compare to America.

I've never lost my passion for singing, and my goal was to always grow and improve as a singer. I wanted to get better each year, and I'm thankful to say that my voice is even stronger today than it was when I was 31 years old.

I'm also thankful for the Oaks who came before us. The early groups were wonderful and had it not been for Jim Hammill before me, Noel Fox before Richard, Smitty Gatlin before Duane and Little Willie Wynn before Joe, the four of us would never have gotten the chance to enjoy the fame and fortune that came our way. Those guys, and the other earlier members all paved the way for us.

We are lifetime members of the Grand Ole Opry, and I think it would be nice if we could still get together to sing on the Opry a few times each year, even after the Oaks retire. But when the Oak Ridge Boys finish touring, I will continue to sing, travel and perform with my sons. If people invite me to sing somewhere, I'll be there. When the Oaks park their bus, I'm going to be on the road with my kids.

Governor Jimmie Davis performed until he was 100. He lived to be 101 years old, so I figure I can go another 20 years. I think it will be pretty cool to be up on a stage, singing when I'm 101.

I think everyone should seek new visions. When you reach one goal, go after another. You want to keep growing in life...mentally, emotionally, physically, and spiritually. The Native Americans, the holy men and medicine men taught that we have four sides. Those are your mental, emotional, physical, and spiritual sides. You need to honor the four directions and need to keep your balance in all four, and if you don't it throws everything off.

I want to do more concerts with my sons. I want to showcase their talents, expose and promote them to a new and larger audience. I'm a huge fan of my sons and I'm proud of all of them.

When I sing and play today with my sons, it is a soothing and healing time for all of us. I feel a genuine warm spirit when I'm with them. Of course, Chris, Rusty, Craig and I spent a lot of time together, touring the country back in the '80s and '90s. I'm sure this time around, we probably won't be quite as rowdy as we were during The Goldens days. We've all grown a little bit since then.

I'm happy to be close friends with my sons. I totally enjoy being around them anytime. Now that Solomon has become a young man, I hope that we can spend more time together. I enjoy his company so much, and I want to be available to help him in any way I can.

When you get old enough that your kids ask you for your advice, and then they become your best friends, it is a great blessing. My dad didn't have a lot, but he was willing to help me at any time. Over the years, I have been willing to help my sons when they needed help in any way. Fatherhood is a lifetime commitment, and it's a lifetime of joy. I love seeing my kids grow and do well, and I love being able to help them if they need something.

I also enjoy my grandkids. Being a grandparent is like parenthood all over again. Being a grandparent really opens up that special part of your heart again. When your kids have a baby, it's like a double joy. And when your grandchild's diapers need changing, you can hand them back to their parents!

I'm fortunate that I've lived long enough to be able to teach my grandchildren some of the things that are important in life, like being honest, having integrity, being a good neighbor and doing unto others as you would have them do unto you. I enjoy being around my grandkids and now my great grandchildren. One of the great blessings of my life has been my family.

When my son Solomon comes to visit, when I have to take him back to the airport and put him on a plane, I now understand how my dad felt when I would bring my little boys to visit him in Alabama. When we would get in the car to leave, Daddy would be crying, as he begged me to move back.

My father always said, "Come back home, son." I told him, "One day I will, Dad. When it's over with the Oaks, when I feel that we've done all we can do, I won't stay in Nashville. I will come back home." I told him the truth, and I will keep my word to him. I will end up back home in Alabama.

I now own the old homeplace where I was raised, just outside Brewton. I've spent the last couple years fixing it up. I can look out the window, across the field, and can see the spot where I was born. My sister lives across the road and she watches over the property when I'm gone.

I love my home at "Golden Era" in Hendersonville, and I plan to continue living there for a while. But I always knew that when the Oaks retired, I would move back to Brewton. I already spend a lot of time at my childhood home. To be able to have a homeplace to come back to is a wonderful blessing. When I pull into the driveway, I am taken back 7 decades. I get a tremendous comfort as a thousand memories flood through my mind.

It was there that I grew up in peace and quiet. And it was there that I had the first visions of my future. When I was a teenager, riding up and down the cotton and peanut fields, I could see where I wanted to go and who I wanted to be. I was never discouraged by hard times or setbacks. I knew what I wanted to do.

The old house is a lot quieter these days, and a little sadder because so many family and friends are gone. But I am content to just sit outside by myself, alone with my thoughts and memories. As I fixed up and updated my old home, I could almost hear my father saying, "Come back home, son." I am thankful that I'm finally able to fulfill my promise to my dad.

I sing lead on the Oaks' song, "Time Has Made a Change in Me." Is that true? Have I changed over time? I think we do change with the years. We all grow, and we try to learn from our mistakes. If I've learned from every mistake I ever made, I must be the smartest man on earth.

I believe in God. I have a deep faith and believe in a Supreme being. If it hadn't been for the hand of God in my life, I shudder to think about where I might be. As I look back on my life, I realize that my parents and grandparent's prayers helped get me through many situations. I would be in the middle of certain things that I allowed myself to get into, and I knew that my parents and grandparent's prayers were protecting me through some dangerous times.

I have been weak in my life. But my faith has always been strong, and my faith continues to get stronger. I wouldn't be anything without my faith. When I walk out to sing every night, I put my trust in God that he will give me the strength, power, and ability to sing as good as I possibly can.

So now you know the real William Lee Golden. For a man of few words, I seem to have filled up this entire book.

Thank you for taking the time to get to know the man behind the beard...and thank you for your friendship and support through the years. Love and God Bless You. WLG

PARTING SONG

When I think of William Lee Golden, a few descriptions come to mind: Original. Gentle. Kind. Multi-talented. Humble. Energetic. Dreamer. Honest.

Yes, William is an original. He is a true one-of-a-kind. But beneath his very "cool" look is one of the kindest and gentlest men in the world. He could give Mister Rogers a run for his money when it comes to being gentle and kind.

While most of us are lucky to find one thing we are good at, William has many talents. Of course, his singing gets most of the attention, but he is also an incredible photographer and artist. But no matter how much fame and fortune he has achieved, William refused to let it change him. He just does not see himself as a star. He has no idea what a legend he is.

At the age of 82, William has more energy than most 28-year-old men. And he needs that energy as he continues to pursue new dreams. William should give seminars on "pursuing your dreams." Over the past year, William had a couple dreams. One was to write the book you are now holding. The other was to record an album with his sons. That turned into three albums! While many people spent most of 2020 locked down in their homes, William was doing the greatest work of his life.

But if I had to choose just one word to describe William, I would say, "honest." William is one of the most honest men I have ever met. I learned very quickly that you should never ask William a question unless you wanted a totally honest answer. Over 9 months, I asked William every question I could come up with...hundreds. Many of those were quite personal. Some were prying and not for the faint of heart. William never flinched. He answered everything I threw at him.

I became a fan of the Oak Ridge Boys when I was just a boy, and I met William Lee for the first time 34 years ago. For most of those years, I lived in Illinois, where I worked as a country music D.J., before becoming a television news reporter and anchor. At least once a year, my wife and I would take a vacation to Nashville, and during each trip, we would go out to Hendersonville to drive by William's home. Like many other tourists, we'd get out and take a photo in front of his gate and next to his famous "spirit tree" that looked like him.

Almost a decade ago, when I became news anchor for the RFD TV Network in Nashville, my family bought a home just down the road from William Lee. William has always been one of my all-time musical heroes, and when I started my writing career, he became my main goal. I dreamed of helping him write his autobiography. But it would take me six years to finally convince him to do it. During that time, I wrote books with Ronnie McDowell, Johnny Lee, Moe Bandy, Jimmy Capps, Lulu Roman, Larry Black and Misty Rowe.

After my fourth release, I approached William and said, "I sure would like to help you write your story, William." He stroked his beard and smiled, "That could be interesting." But that was as far as our conversation went. I continued to work with other artists and released 3 more books; then, William's son Chris got involved. When Chris saw the success I was having, he called William and told him he should do a book with me. A few minutes later, William called me. Thank you so much Chris! It wouldn't have gotten done without you!

Chris was also instrumental in another way. His mother, William's first wife, Frogene, was fighting terminal cancer. I had told Chris that while I had always dreamed of writing the book, I really did not want to do it unless I was able to include Frogene. She had been there at the beginning of everything, when she and William were just teenagers. She remembered many stories William had forgotten long ago, and the book would be totally different and much less complete without her.

In June of 2020, Chris and Rusty were taking care of Frogene at her home in Brewton, Alabama. Chris called me and said, "If you want to do an interview with Mom, you need to get down here tomorrow, because she doesn't have much time left."

I will never forget how Chris and Rusty allowed my wife and me to be a part of that very personal and intimate time with their Mother. During that time, Frogene shared one memory after another. With each one, she laughed and she cried. At the end of one long interview, I told Frogene, "By doing this, you are giving William a wonderful gift." She smiled her beautiful smile and said, "Well, it's my last gift to him. I still love him very much."

Frogene gave William that gift during the last week of her life. Thank you Frogene. I wouldn't have done the book without you. I also wouldn't have done it without William's sons, Chris, Rusty, Craig, and Solomon. I thank all of you for sharing your time and memories with me.

Of course, this book wouldn't have been complete without the other "boys"...the Oak Ridge Boys. Thank you to Duane, Joe, and Richard. Thank you for taking the time to interview with me, but also thank you for all the years of joy, and thousands of memories you have given to me, my wife, and daughter as we have cheered you on over the last 4 decades.

My thanks to Jim Halsey. Mr. Halsey, you are a true legend. I wanted so much for this book to get your blessing, and you will never know how thrilled I was when you called to say how great you thought it was.

My sincere thanks to all of William's friends and fans who worked me into their schedule. Thanks to you, this book became something I hope you will all be proud of.

To Simone…what a wonderful person you are. I thank you for all your help. We also couldn't have done it without you. Thank you for welcoming me into your home, especially during the scary lockdown of 2020.

Finally, to William Lee: William, this has been not only a highlight of my career, but also a highlight of my life. There were many days over the past year, as we would visit or just sit and listen to music, that I would silently think to myself, "This is a dream come true." Many days, as I left your driveway, I would pray out loud, "Thank you, Lord. Thank you for giving me this miracle."

After all those years as a fan, driving by your home, and even stopping to take a photo by your gate…and now I was behind the gate, inside your living room, becoming a close friend. I truly consider that a miracle from God.

Through his entire life, William Lee has been a dreamer. He still is. One day, as he was talking about how we should all go after our dreams, I stopped him and said, "William, you are preaching to the choir. I had a dream of writing this book with you, and I did everything I could to make that dream come true." And now that we've come to the last page of the book, as William would say, "It's time to get a new dream to go after."

— Scot England